KELLY DAY

FINANCIAL SERVICES, LLC

12205 Station Road • Columbia Station, OH 44028

Cell: 216-225-9075 • Fax: 440-236-8564

e-mail: vschmitz@investonesco.com

www.kellydayfs.com

Securities offered through The O.N. Equity Sales Company, Member FINRA/SIPC, One Financial Way, Cincinnati, OH 45242 513.794.6794. Investment Advisory services offered through ON Investment Management Company

PRAISE FOR *SMART RETIREMENT*

"I believe that many tax professionals will think differently and advise their clients differently after learning about the Strategic Movement Around Retirement Taxation®. The concept of tax arbitrage and the diversification of taxable distribution sources is really straightforward and not hard to understand. I've just never seen it described anywhere else like it is here in the *SMART Retirement* book."

—STEVE MAGNONE, CPA

"I've read a lot of textbooks while getting my masters in taxation, yet this is the book that contains the most actionable and useful information about postretirement income taxation for a retiree and those approaching retirement. It's incredible to have this valuable tool available to help my clients understand how the Strategic Movement Around Retirement Taxation® increases the value of their money in retirement and enhances their income, wealth, and legacy."

—ZACH HESSELBAUM, ESQ., LLM

"Matt, you have done it again! Your previous work has enhanced the lives of countless Americans, and no doubt this will too. Being in an industry that seems to have forgotten that, without clients, we are all out of a job, it's a comfort to know that there are some people who really do care and share information that can have a positive impact both now and for future generations.

As you read in *SMART Retirement* about what the 'big boys' are doing with their money, you might think, 'Yeah, but look at how many millions they have.' What this book teaches us is that although the 'big boys' may have more zeroes in their account balances, the principles around tax-advantaged planning are the same for all of us. I hope this book does for you what it has done for me and my clients."

—RON CAMPBELL, CFP, CAMPBELL FINANCIAL SERVICES

"Once you understand the three dates that completely altered the face and future of the American retirement system, you immediately know that old-world ideas are not going to solve these new-world problems. SMART is the solution that creates a true private reserve wealth strategy for my clients."

—TOM BORIS, ESQ., ELDER LAW OFFICES OF SHIELDS & BORIS

"For me, SMART's value is truly found in the attention it gives to the preservation of family wealth. I'm a family-oriented person, and modern financial planning has turned a blind eye to the preservation of principal—something that was ingrained in my thinking and beliefs growing up in Western Pennsylvania. I believe you shouldn't spend what you've saved; instead, you should live off the interest your savings earn. SMART has that same effect but with better economics and lower tax rates along with a plan for these low-yield times. SMART is more than a strategy; it's a shift in how lawyers, advisors, and tax professionals need to think when representing their clients. I highly recommend this book."

—JIM SHIELDS, ESQ., ELDER LAW OFFICES OF SHIELDS & BORIS

"For the past twelve years, our firm has consistently looked to Matt Zagula to help with the design and development of outstanding client solutions by combining financial products with innovative trust designs. Throughout our long relationship, Matt has shown himself to be a man of vision and integrity. His latest book on the Strategic Movement Around Retirement Taxation® is a must-read for anyone over the age of fifty."

—RICK L. LAW, SENIOR PARTNER AT LAW ELDERLAW, ESTATE, ASSET PROTECTION AND RETIREMENT TAX ATTORNEYS

"I've spent my entire career in the financial services and insurance industry so the concept of actuarial arbitrage really resonated with me. Once I understood the value in the 'math' of SMART, compared to normal Wall Street and banker math, I became a true believer in SMART. Do yourself a favor—get SMART and learn the truth about money."

—SCOTT LUSTER, INSURANCE EXECUTIVE

"I love this book. After more than thirty years in the financial services industry, it's great to read something truly innovative. This book gives real hardworking people the tools they need to design a SMART strategy with their savings by taking advantage of techniques that the financial elite has been using for years! SMART does not offer a traditional view of financial planning, but once you learn what America's most wealthy individuals and their families are doing with their money, it only makes sense to be SMART about your own retirement planning."

—NANCY BRUNETTI, OCEAN CREST FINANCIAL

SMART
RETIREMENT

SMART
RETIREMENT

DISCOVER THE
STRATEGIC MOVEMENT AROUND
RETIREMENT TAXATION®

MATT ZAGULA

ForbesBooks

Published by ForbesBooks, Charleston, South Carolina.
Member of Advantage Media Group.

ForbesBooks is a registered trademark, and the ForbesBooks colophon is a trademark of Forbes Media, LLC.

Printed in the United States of America.

10 9 8 7 6 5

ISBN: 978-0-9983655-9-6
LCCN: 2017936860

Cover design by George Stevens.

Advantage Media Group is proud to be a part of the Tree Neutral® program. Tree Neutral offsets the number of trees consumed in the production and printing of this book by taking proactive steps such as planting trees in direct proportion to the number of trees used to print books. To learn more about Tree Neutral, please visit **www.treeneutral.com**.

Since 1917, the Forbes mission has remained constant. Global Champions of Entrepreneurial Capitalism. ForbesBooks exists to further that aim by bringing the Stories, Passion, and Knowledge of top thought leaders to the forefront. ForbesBooks brings you The Best in Business. To be considered for publication, please visit **www.forbesbooks.com**.

TABLE OF CONTENTS

FOREWORD

I know it is unusual for a medical doctor to write a foreword to a financial book. After all, doctors are known as traditionally bad financial managers. But I know how intertwined your financial well-being is to your health. After all, I've authored or coauthored four number-one *New York Times* bestsellers on aging, each of which describe how important managing financial stress is to your health (yes, we will all have financial stress, no matter how much money you have), as well as coauthoring with Jean Chatzky of NBC Today the recent *New York Times* bestseller, *AgeProof: Living Longer Without Running Out Of Money or Breaking a Hip.*

The unusualness of a doctor writing a foreword on a financial book should underscore for you, the reader, just how unusual this book is. The *SMART Retirement* system is eye opening in its approach, enviable in its lucidity, and *awesome* in delivering actionable information. Now, a medical doctor is rarely, if ever, that enthusiastic about a book or anything financial, even when it involves maneuvers that help you maximize your after-tax income decades from now.

So what was different about this book? Well, first, no financial advisor has ever focused my attention so clearly on the net or after-tax income I will receive after retirement. No advisor or planner has ever told me about how the government has laws that teach me the way they want me to receive those monies. And until now, no financial advisor has told me of these connections and pathways to more spendable income in retirement the way that Matt Zagula does in this book. That clarity and those insights, ending with actionable steps is what makes it, in strictly nonmedical terms, *awesome*.

For the healthiest body in the world won't stay that way if you're frazzled, with about six figures worth of debt, or worried about whether your retirement funds will fund your lifestyle. (I dislike using the word "retirement," as I think you will always stay active, just change your focus on what activity you want to pursue and why you pursue it. But for this foreword, I'll go along and use "retirement" to indicate that period of time after you stop the job you had that led to accumulating money.)

When I started reading this book, I realized this was a bright, eye-opening approach. It wasn't about how to accumulate dollars (spend less, save more, I know) but about how to position that money to have the maximum amount to spend every year in retirement and still leave a legacy. It focused my attention so clearly on the after-tax income I will receive, which seems so obvious a goal *I began to wonder why no one else had ever mentioned it to me.*

SMART Retirement isn't just about accumulating money, something that Matt likens to climbing up the mountain, which is hard enough. It is really about how to maximize what you have to spend from that hard step of accumulation—so that the difficulty in accumulating can be worth the effort and the trip down the mountain can be rich, fun, and all you dreamed it could be. Although Matt doesn't promise it, following his methods, you will be able to do more of what you dreamed of doing.

You see, what's different about this book is that it isn't about how to invest in any one type of investment to maximize that accumulation. No, instead Matt takes you through a *SMART Retirement* process that provides you with a systematic approach to getting what you want and need out of your retirement so that you can be comfortable and less taxed. He then helps you compound these tax-advantaged dollars, using straightforward math, to leave a meaningful legacy—money that your surviving spouse, children, and grandchildren will need. In Matt's words, "SMART will guide you in the Strategic Movement Around Retirement Taxation®, teaching you how to take advantage of tax and actuarial" opportunities.

Matt presents these opportunities with a crispness and clearness that even a doctor can understand. He shows you how to do this the way the big companies do when they provide for their CEO's retirement, not with a 401(k) or stock options but with what the US government wants you to do. Yes, the government wants you to own a home—that's why it made mortgage interest deductible on your taxes. And the US government *wants* you to delay Social Security withdrawal—that's why it increases the amount you receive about 8 percent per year after age sixty-two. But I didn't realize the government *wants* me to own a cash-value-building, low-death-benefit life insurance policy till I read it here. And that the government makes it tax-advantaged to access the funds in that policy after it is paid up.

The reason a *SMART Retirement* plan is important—right now—is that the world is in the middle of a pretty large shift when it comes to aging. How old do you think you'll get to be? Seventy-seven? Eighty-four? Ninety-two? One hundred? Whatever number popped into your head, chances are that you're about as wrong as a steady diet of junk food. You're going to live longer than whatever number you picked (even longer than preservative-filled junk foods, some of which can last in your refrigerator for years, by the way). Just consider this: in the past three decades, life expectancy in the United States has jumped for men from seventy to seventy-nine and for women from seventy-seven to eighty-three.

Over the last hundred or so years, one innovation after another has prolonged life: the tuberculosis vaccine (1921), penicillin (1929), high-blood-pressure meds (1947), the surgeon general's warning on cigarettes (1969), seat belt laws (1984), tests for inflammation becoming routine (1986), vaccines for preventing cervical and throat cancer (2004) and for treating a specific cancer (2006). With so many life-threatening problems not needing as much attention, medicine can focus on managing chronic conditions such as arthritis, asthma, diabetes, or osteoporosis. Even some types of cancer and HIV/AIDS are now considered manageable. The result? Life goes on longer than ever before, with you being able to live younger no matter what your age. It's like cars now lasting two hundred thousand miles on average, compared to sixty thousand miles in 1970.

While the change in longevity should be exciting, the truth is that longevity comes with a price. Because we're living longer, it's more expensive to fund retirement. That's true even if you're in good shape. Surveys from financial institutions note that running out of money before running out of time is by far our biggest financial fear. One survey even found that running short of funds is a bigger fear than death. Going the distance means we all need a new set of skills, new strategies, and a new way of thinking to have that money. And, as Matt Zagula keeps pointing out, it isn't just that you saved enough but that you put it in the right vehicles at the right time to maximize the amount of money that your savings provides you to live on "after taxes."

This book is about giving you the power to take the ride of your life for the second part of your life—all without limping around with duct tape over your rear bumper. Matt Zagula is clear and generous with his knowledge. He even suggests books to read after this one. He presents a plan to thrive financially through that second part of life.

When you read this book, you'll see that Matt gives you the needed pieces and the knowledge to solve the puzzle of "retirement" planning and tax arbitrage. Matt makes the strategies clear, with well-defined action steps. And the book is even fun to read, and that is saying a lot for a financial planning book. In the end having enough money to last is romantic, which means this book may even improve your love life, and that's good for your health too.

MICHAEL F. ROIZEN, MD

Chief Wellness Officer (CWO)
Roizen Family Chair, the Wellness Institute of the Cleveland Clinic

ABOUT THIS BOOK

The world can be a scary place these days. A lot has changed. Yet, despite the changes in our world, economy, and political atmosphere, recommendations from traditional financial planners and the investment advising community have pretty much stayed the same. When the market is down, we still hear the endless refrain of, "Hold on, it'll come back." When the market is up, we're consistently told that we should "buy into this strength."

This book is dedicated to questioning the financial sense in believing we can continue to solve new-world problems with the same old answers. I'll take a very firm position and tell you that we cannot do that—continually recycle old ideas—and expect to be successful with them. Instead, I want to offer you, the much-appreciated reader of this book, insight into a different way to view your planning as you build toward retirement. For those of you who are already in retirement, I'll encourage you to focus on what really matters . . . the money that comes to you each month *after* your taxes are paid.

The SMART retirement planning process, which stands for the **S**trategic **M**ovement **A**round **R**etirement **T**axation®, is a system I developed so that my clients, and the advisors who seek my counsel, can remain focused on their primary goal of achieving the greatest net after-tax retirement income without cannibalizing their principal.

In these low interest rate, yield-strapped times, the financial planning and advisory community are quick to throw in the towel on their clients' end-of-life principal balances in favor of what has been popularized as *safe money* advising or *income planning*. These are red-flag terms that translate into: *we will use your assets to promise you a lifetime income but guarantee nothing for the preservation of your principal for your family after you die.*

Years ago, I worked as a consultant for companies that promote these types of plans to advisors. What I found was that their marketing pitches were parallel to an airline's pre-flight instruction. You know the one—"In the unlikely event of a loss of cabin pressure, panels above your seat will open revealing oxygen masks. Reach up and pull a mask toward you. *Secure your own mask first before helping others.*" It was like they were telling their clients to worry only about their own income—not their family, not their legacy, and not the security of their capital.

Soon this became the slogan of the income-planning, safe-money marketers who promoted these ideas and concepts to advisors desperately searching for yield for their clients. Eventually, we started to honestly believe it was acceptable to just focus on income through-out retirement—which alone is just not enough. As you'll later learn, even reputable research firms, such as Morningstar, are now finding that the safe withdrawal rate from your retirement funds is equal to just 2.8 percent per year—and the way they define "safe" is simply making sure you don't completely run out of money before you run out of life. Think I'm kidding? In their January 21, 2013, study, "Low Bond Yields and Safe Portfolio Withdrawal Rates," Morningstar makes it clear that their definition of success is not running completely out of money in retirement. It's shocking to believe that, based on their findings, if you take just $28,000 per year from a $1 million IRA with 40 percent of its holdings in stock, you have a 90 percent chance of not going broke (account value to $0).[1] Again, keep in mind success means *not going broke*. It doesn't mean keeping your $1,000,000 of principal; it simply means not going to $0! Weird definition of success, isn't it?

You might think that reducing your risk and shifting assets from stocks to bonds could possibly solve this income problem, but that doesn't seem to be the case. Morningstar's expert research team found that if you drop the stock market exposure on a $1 million IRA from 40 percent to 20 percent, it actually *reduces* the distribution rate from 2.8 percent to 2.7 percent. Of course, this also means that doubling your stock market exposure adds only a paltry one tenth of 1 percent to your potential retirement income distributions. It makes you wonder if it's worth the risk.

It's hard to justify, at least in my conservative mind, accepting this level of risk for only $27,000 to $28,000 per year from a $1 million IRA *before* taxes. And let's say you're like millions of Americans who don't have $1 million saved. Let's say you're sitting on a $100,000 retirement account balance. That gives you just $2,700 to $2,800 per year—again, *before* taxes!

All of this information is probably making you question whether you can achieve an attractive retirement income with the money you have saved. You may even be asking yourself if it's reasonable to believe you can acquire enough from now until retirement to achieve a reasonable postretirement lifestyle. The challenges presented by this prolonged low-yield environment paved the way for the rise of the income-planning niche within the financial advisory and planning industry. These planners offered a solution with their ironically named

1   David Blanchett, Michael Finke, and Wade Pfau, "Low Bond Yields and Safe Portfolio Withdrawal Rates," Morningstar, January 21, 2013.

safe-money strategies. I'd agree it solved the low-yield dilemma, but at what cost? Their client's principal—maybe a portion of it or maybe all of it, depending on how long their client lived.

I believe the safe-money, income-planning crew missed a few very important realities. One of the biggest things they missed is the fact that the oxygen mask we put on ourselves first *needs to be passed on to the people we love most.* Every single day I look at my fourteen-year-old son Charlie, and I cringe, knowing that the future he faces is not an easy one. I think about these facts:

- The days of defined benefit plans, where a company provides a monthly pension when you retire from service, are gone!

- Younger workers today rely solely on their 401(k) plans. You'll learn as we progress through this book that 401(k) plans provide a useful tool for the accumulation of money but are poor vehicles for the distribution of that money once we reach retirement. You'll learn exactly why this is and how to start fixing these issues now—even if you are already in retirement! The 401(k) is like chocolate cake—a small piece isn't bad, but if you go for the whole cake, you'll end up miserable.

- It is our responsibility to learn and then expose how banks and brokerage firms use fuzzy math to "help" us fund and plan our future (and, yes, the sarcasm here is intended). The banks are taking advantage of us, and it's our job to become informed and take back control. As you read, you'll learn the right way to calculate interest on loans, how misleading an average rate of return can be, and why your rate of return in retirement is, at most, a half-truth.

You'll learn for yourself that *when* you earn money is much more important than *what* you earn in retirement.

- Social Security is cooked. Visit their website and see for yourself. Some time on or about 2034, the system becomes insolvent, which is just a nice word for financially broke and a system that is broken. But don't take it from me, take it directly from the Social Security website:

> *The OASDI reserves are projected to grow in 2017 because total income ($1,014 billion) will exceed total cost ($955 billion). This year's report indicates that annual OASDI income, including payments of interest to the trust funds from the General Fund, will continue to exceed annual cost every year until 2022, increasing the nominal value of combined OASDI trust fund asset reserves. Social Security's cost is projected to exceed its non-interest income by $27 billion in 2017, and annual non-interest income deficits will persist through 2091. The trust fund ratio (the ratio of projected reserves to annual cost) will continue to decline gradually (Chart E), as it has since 2008, despite this nominal balance increase. Beginning in 2022, net redemptions of trust fund asset reserves with General Fund payments will be required until projected depletion of these reserves in 2034.[2]*

My goal is for the SMART retirement planning process to empower you to look past the slogans and half-truths being thrown at us every day, funded by the big advertising dollars paid by America's

---

2   "A SUMMARY OF THE 2017 ANNUAL REPORTS," Social Security Administration, www.ssa.gov/oact/trsum/.

big banks and Wall Street. It's to help you put your family's oxygen mask on without endangering your own financial breath. It's to ensure that your postretirement phase is as comfortable as you expected it to be while you were saving money in preretirement.

So what is the SMART retirement planning process? First, it's a systematic approach to getting what you want and need out of your retirement so that you can be comfortable and *less taxed*. It then goes on to help you compound these tax-advantaged dollars, using straightforward math, to leave a meaningful legacy—money that your surviving spouse, children, and grandchildren will *need*.

SMART will guide you in the **S**trategic **M**ovement **A**round **R**etirement **T**axation®, teaching you how to take advantage of tax and actuarial arbitrage opportunities. These opportunities will become clearer and clearer as you read through the material.

Ultimately, you'll be introduced to the way our country's most successful and celebrated investor, Warren Buffett, continues to compound wealth within his holding company, Berkshire Hathaway, by effectively understanding the profit potential of *float*. Float has been such a significant wealth warehouse for Buffett that he specifically uses the term forty-six times in his 2015 letter to shareholders of Berkshire Hathaway.

If Buffett has such enthusiasm for this opportunity, I would imagine those of us who are motivated by getting the most out of our hard-earned money would too. I'd think we'd be willing to take the time to learn how to use a version of this powerful concept within our personal finances.

At the end of the day, we all want to secure a better financial future for ourselves and our families. That's what SMART is ultimately about. It's not a secret scheme to get rich or a hyped-up, shady tax loophole. It's about good, old-fashioned smart planning for a tricky new economic outlook.

If you're ready to invest the time to work hard, study, and get SMART, then you're ready to learn about and integrate the Strategic Movement Around Retirement Taxation® into your overall financial plan.

ACKNOWLEDGMENTS

I want to take this opportunity to acknowledge the significant contribution a few individuals have made to the world of finance. Often, hindsight is 20/20 and I believe many will look back and realize their retirement could have been better if they had been exposed to these two gifted thought leaders and authors.

First, I want to recognize Nelson Nash, the creator of the Infinite Banking Concept and author of *Becoming Your Own Banker*. Nelson is a self-taught Austrian economist who goes beyond the theory of money, economy, and national wealth and literally brings it to your kitchen table. His book should be mandatory reading starting in the eighth grade and required each and every year thereafter. With his Infinite Banking Concept, you never really graduate, you just get better as time goes on. It is, without any hesitation, one of the best books on personal finance ever written. You should read it as soon as you finish this book.

Next, I'd highly recommend you read Barry James Dyke's book *Guaranteed Income: A Risk-Free Guide to Retirement*. Barry is one of the finest financial researchers you'd ever have the privilege to learn from. It speaks volumes that the former US Comptroller General David M. Walker wrote the foreword to Barry's book. I give a copy of Barry's book to every single one of my new clients as they go through my SMART retirement planning process. With so much *mis*information out there both online and offline (through the media, which serves their advertisers and their own financial interests), Barry's book brings the truth, proves it, and then reveals what the SMART money people *actually do* with their money. It's an eye opener when you see what financial industry CEOs do with their own wealth compared to what their companies do when they offer to manage yours. I'll refer to Barry's research a number of times in my book, but it is not a substitute for reading *Guaranteed Income*.

I'm blessed to work with a number of extremely talented asset management firms that now realize the importance of recapitalizing the retirement wealth lost to income in these low-yield times for the next generation. These advisors continue to amaze me as they grow in their knowledge of bringing a holistic approach to building wealth, distributing income, and implementing a total wealth management process for their clients.

I am equally blessed to work with some of the most successful multidisciplinary law firms in America. These talented counselors not only navigate the complexities of trust law, estate planning, income tax, and estate tax laws for their clients but they also understand how to synergistically weave suitable financial products into their clients' plans, enhancing the benefits of the trusts they create and making financial products work more efficiently toward the clients' goals than would otherwise be possible with the financial product alone.

Finally, I want to thank and acknowledge my hardworking team at Zagula Management, the conscientious, client-first-focused advisors at First Financial Strategies, our office building suite mates, my editors, and a special thanks to Yolander Prinzel, who took every concept and word I wrote and made it a lot better.

CHAPTER 1

THE WORLD IS CHANGING. ARE YOU?

I'm going to say something that I bet will come as no shock to you but which still needs to be said: the world is changing. Look at our debt, our national and international politics, and the economies of all the great nations around the world. It's a crazy time filled with unprecedented problems, innovative but largely untested solutions, and general insecurity about what the future brings.

If there's one thing we know, it's that we can't fix new-world problems with old-world solutions. That would be like trying to treat cancer with a combination of leeches and snake oil. We have to adapt and find alternative, progressive solutions that factor in all the changes surrounding us and that help to insulate our money and our future from what may come.

There are three dates that changed the face and future of the American retirement system. Because of these dates, it doesn't matter which candidate you vote for or which political party controls what branch of the government. Although all the politicians today want to make it about the vote—telling you that if you vote for their candidate this-and-that is going to get better, that it's Obama's fault for absolutely everything that's wrong, or maybe that everything we're dealing with now is Donald Trump's fault—the reality is that these three dates I'll mention are what *really* changed the face and future of the American retirement system forever. It doesn't matter what person holds which office, these dates, and their impact on the future, cannot be changed by any politician. They're just facts. Let's walk through what they are.

THREE IMPORTANT DATES

The first retirement-system-changing date was on January 1, 2008. It was on this day that the first baby boomer turned sixty-two years old and qualified to take early Social Security distributions. Now, if it was just one baby boomer, that would be fine—but it's not. In fact, every day after that date, an average of ten thousand baby boomers turn sixty-two and, as such, qualify for early Social Security distributions.

The second date that changed the American retirement system was January 1, 2011. If you're quick at math you've already figured out why this date matters—it's because that's the date that the first baby boomer turned sixty-five and not only qualified for full Social Security benefits but, if they weren't still working at a company that offered health insurance and they were retired, also had a new primary healthcare provider: Medicare. And guess what? Every day after that date we've had an average of ten thousand baby boomers turning sixty-five and qualifying for the same benefits. Imagine that—ten thousand new potential Social Security and Medicare recipients *every single day.*[3] Never before have we had such a large, seemingly unending stream of people ready to tap into retirement and health-care programs all at one time.

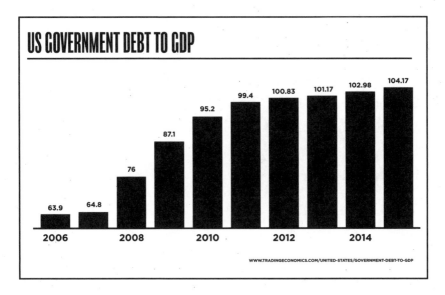

US GOVERNMENT DEBT TO GDP

63.9 · 64.8 · 76 · 87.1 · 95.2 · 99.4 · 100.83 · 101.17 · 102.98 · 104.17

2006 · 2008 · 2010 · 2012 · 2014

WWW.TRADINGECONOMICS.COM/UNITED-STATES/GOVERNMENT-DEBT-TO-GDP

Fig. 1

So what does this do to our country? Take a moment to review Figure 1. I think it tells a very important story. But before I get into that, let me start by stating that I believe taxes are going up—way up, over the long term. It's important for you to know that. We may see lower rates for a while (which, interestingly, actually makes starting a SMART plan now even more beneficial), but ultimately the debts must be paid—and that means taxes are going to rise. I have a belief, and it's a planning bias, that traditional planning is failing because it is not willing to acknowledge and accept this fact. That's right—this is a belief but it's supported by facts. Look at Figure 1. Notice the comparatively small numbers in 2006 and 2007 and then the conspicuous spike in 2008. What does it all

3   "Baby Boomers Retire," Pew Research Center, December 29, 2010, http://www.pewresearch. org/daily-number/baby-boomers-retire/.

mean? Well, this graph represents the percentage of the US government debt to the entire gross domestic product (GDP) of our country. This is all of the economic activity that goes on and what percentage of that economic activity represents our government debt. In 2008, when those first baby boomers had the opportunity to take Social Security, well . . . some of them did—and it spiked our ratio of debt to GDP. That's what you see reflected in that graph. The next year, even more eligible baby boomers signed up to receive their promised benefit. Of course, by 2010 even more did. Now, in 2011 we see more of a sustainable curve going on, because just like health insurance, costs go up a little bit more over time. This is the phenomenon that I believe indicates that taxes must be adjusted over the long haul.

HOW TAXES ADJUST

Taxes are adjusted in one of two ways, if not both. The first is to raise the tax rates. This is literally where the government tax authority just says, "Hey, the rate was 15 percent, now it's 20." So rate increases are something that I'm anticipating will eventually occur.

The second way taxes are raised is through what I call *rollbacks*. Let's just imagine a service right now that's paid for by Medicare. Next year, Medicare says, "Instead of paying providers directly, we're going to reimburse you, and we're going to pay less for that service." When Medicare pays less, a retiree's supplemental insurance has to make up the difference. I can tell you, though, that they aren't going to do this out of the kindness of their hearts. During the next year, when that supplemental insurance incurs this added cost, the expense has to be reimbursed and paid back to the insurance company in the form of higher premiums *paid by the senior who's supposed to be receiving all these promised benefits.*

So when I say taxes are going up, and they have the potential to go way up, it's because I believe that the percentage rate of taxation will increase, and I also believe that promises that were made will be rolled back or potentially even reneged on.

In my area of the country, the Rust Belt where there's a lot of manufacturing, we know that pension plans and health insurance, what were commonly referred to as *legacy costs*, literally put many of these companies out of business. Unlike the government, these companies actually did try to put money aside in order to meet their obligations to their employees. The companies then discovered, painfully, that it was really hard to keep up with the costs and distribution obligations when people started taking money out.

So the government, suddenly saddled with a lot more retirees than they're used to, makes this same discovery—but it's even worse. Unlike business owners, the government never even put any money aside. The more people who call in and say, "Hey, these are the promises you made and we want to collect on this," the more money our government has to either print or tax to get. Ultimately, this results in higher taxation.

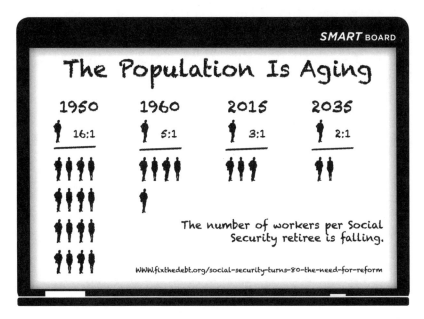

Fig. 2

5

This isn't a problem that can be solved politically. This is an age demographic issue, and make no mistake about it, our population is aging. Back in the 1950s, there were sixteen workers for every one Social Security recipient. That allowed us to spread the responsibility to a wide number of workers so they didn't really feel the pinch, and the government could fulfill its promises. Today, our population is aging and we are inching toward a three-to-one ratio—which means we've only got three workers for every one Social Security recipient.[4] So the workers feel the pinch a heck of a lot more, but so far the government can still carry out promises.

How long will the government be able to do that? Possibly for another sixteen years or so. We know this just by looking at the Social Security website, where they clearly disclose that there is a point where the government says the Social Security system simply doesn't work anymore—that it's broken. That time comes in 2034, when reserves are depleted and we have more Social Security recipients than we have workers paying for their benefits. And there is no political solution to this. This is an age demographic issue and an economic issue. It's just undeniable. Again, here's what they have to say about it:

> *The OASDI reserves are projected to grow in 2017 because total income ($1,014 billion) will exceed total cost ($955 billion). This year's report indicates that annual OASDI income, including payments of interest to the trust funds from the General Fund, will continue to exceed annual cost every year until 2022, increasing the nominal value of combined OASDI trust fund asset reserves. Social Security's cost is projected to exceed its non-interest income by $27 billion in*

---

4   "The 2017 Annual Report of the Board of Trustees of the Federal Old-Age and Survivors Insurance and Federal Disability Insurance Trust Funds," July 13, 2017, https://www.ssa.gov/oact/tr/2017/tr2017.pdf

2017, and annual non-interest income deficits will persist through 2091. The trust fund ratio (the ratio of projected reserves to annual cost) will continue to decline gradually (Chart E), as it has since 2008, despite this nominal balance increase. Beginning in 2022, net redemptions of trust fund asset reserves with General Fund payments will be required until projected depletion of these reserves in 2034.[5]

TAXES AND CASH-FLOW PRESSURE

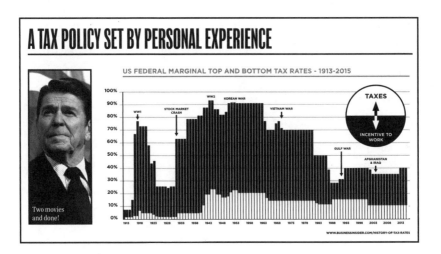

Fig. 3

Taxes *can* go up, even though most people feel like taxes can't get any worse. You probably remember, or certainly have heard of, Ronald Reagan. Many believe that his was one of the greatest economic minds ever to preside over this nation. I would argue that his tax policy seems to have been set primarily by his individual experience. This was a point raised at a recent conference I attended, and when I decided to do some research on Reagan and his earnings, I was

---

5   "A SUMMARY OF THE 2017 ANNUAL REPORTS," Social Security Administration, www.ssa. gov/oact/trsum/.

shocked at what I discovered. Let me explain why. Reagan was the highest-paid movie actor in the early 1940s. If you look at Figure 3, you'll see that at that time, the top marginal tax bracket over $200,000 was 88 percent.[6] If you add in California's state tax, it's said that Reagan was paying over 91 percent in taxes, which meant he had little incentive to make more than two movies a year. In fact, he is quoted as rhetorically asking former Secretary of the Treasury Donald T. Regan what good it would have done him to have filmed a third picture each year. Instead, he would do two movies and then he was done because most of the money he earned above that would have been lost to taxation. So he had no incentive to keep going to the set and making movies and instead chose to "loaf" six months of the year.[7]

You may think we're in high tax periods today, but just take a look at the US federal top marginal and bottom marginal tax bracket from the inception of taxes back in 1913 and you can plainly see that taxes have been much higher than they are now. The higher they go, the less incentive people have to work—and the incentive to work is very important because many of the benefits that were promised to seniors are going to be paid for by younger workers. We can't completely disincentivize them from working, especially since there are only three paying for every one Social Security recipient. But we risk doing just that because we need to raise taxes and likely roll back promised benefits to eventually manage our nation's ever-expanding debt. So we are in a very unique economic time. Once again, the world has changed, and it's not like someone can just fix it and bring

---

6   Henry Blodget, "The Truth about Taxes: Here's How High Today's Rates Really Are," Business Insider, July 12, 2011, http://www.businessinsider.com/history-of-tax-rates.
7   Gerald Strober and Deborah Hart Strober, Reagan: The Man and His Presidency (Houghton Mifflin, 1998).

it back to some normalcy that we understood in the past. It's a new situation.

Now one of the things that always comes up when I'm meeting with a client is what my thoughts are on the market. There was a time when I felt that inflation would make the market go up because things just naturally get more expensive over time. But today, I think that there's a different and more likely scenario going on. My new response is that I think the market is under significant cash-flow pressure, and that cash-flow pressure is going to worsen over time. Here's why:

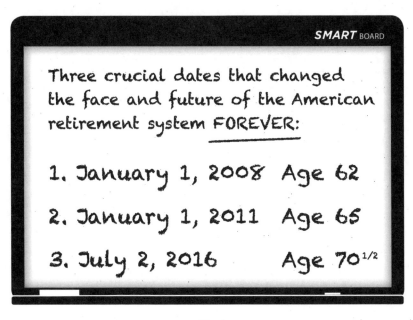

Fig. 4

Remember those three dates we talked about? We've already talked about 2008 and 2011. Now let's talk about the third date, July 2, 2016. What happened on that date? The very first baby boomer hit age 70.5 and was required to begin taking minimum distributions

(RMDs) from certain retirement plans, including the traditional IRA and 401(k) plans. Now, let's talk about why that matters.

THE TROUBLE WITH RMDS

REQUIRED MINIMUM DISTRIBUTION

Table III (Uniform Lifetime)

Age	Distribution Period	Age	Distribution Period	Age	Distribution Period	Age	Distribution Period
70	27.4	82	17.1	94	9.1	106	4.2
71	26.5	83	16.3	95	8.6	107	3.9
72	25.6	84	15.5	96	8.1	108	3.7
73	24.7	85	14.8	97	7.6	109	3.4
74	23.8	86	14.1	98	7.1	110	3.1
75	22.9	87	13.4	99	6.7	111	2.9
76	22.0	88	12.7	100	6.3	112	2.6
77	21.2	89	12.0	101	5.9	113	2.4
78	20.3	90	11.4	102	5.5	114	2.1
79	19.5	91	10.8	103	5.2	115 and over	1.9
80	18.7	92	10.2	104	4.9		
81	17.9	93	9.6	105	4.5		

Once you determine a separate required minimum distribution from each of your traditional IRAs, you can total these minimum amounts and take them from any one or more of your traditional IRAs.

Fig. 5

When you have a tax-deferred retirement account, like the traditional IRA, you avoided paying taxes on the contributions you made over the years. You've also grown your money—again, without taxation. The IRS isn't going to let that go on forever, so at age 70.5 they require participants to begin taking taxable distributions, based on their age, life expectancy, and balance from the prior year. The IRS has a uniform table that tells seniors how much they must take. I've published their table here.

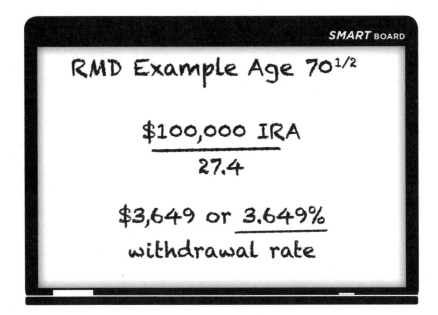

Fig. 6

Essentially, the way it works is you take the account balance from December 31 of the prior year and you divide it by the number in the *Distribution Period* column next to your age. Some people ask me what this number means. It's a joint life expectancy, assuming that your spouse is ten years younger. They call it a uniform table because that's what everybody uses even if you aren't married, widowed, or married to an older spouse.

Now let's convert this into an example to make it easier to understand. Let's say that Mary, a retiree who is 70.5 years old, has $100,000 in her IRA. She must start taking minimum distributions, so according to Figure 6, she must take the balance of her IRA and divide it by 27.4. That means that her distribution now is $3,649 per year. Let's reverse this and consider what percentage of her overall balance that distribution is. In this case, the required distribution of $3,649 divided by $100,000 is 3.649 percent. That seems pretty low, right? It's less than 4 percent, which is what many traditional retirement planners suggest for withdrawals, so maybe the IRS is onto something with their formula!

Or . . . not—because in a minute here, you're going to find out that 3.659 percent is a very large, completely unsustainable distribution rate in today's low-yield environment.

LOW BOND YIELDS AND SAFE PORTFOLIO WITHDRAWAL RATES

January 21, 2013

MORNINGSTAR

Fig. 7

Now maybe some of you have heard of Morningstar, the publishers of the report shown in Figure 7. Morningstar is a leading investment research firm in North America. Their accurate, insightful, unbiased reports are used by countless brokerage firms, planners, asset management firms, and others. In 2013, they published this study of their findings on low yields and safe withdrawal rates from retirement plans. The authors of the study were notable and accomplished PhDs with advanced degrees in economics and finance. They concluded that our ability to avoid running out of money in retirement was based on taking no more than 2.8 percent a year from our accounts.[8] Now just think about that: 2.8 percent. On a $100,000 account for our retiree, Mary, that would be $2,800—quite a difference from the $3,649 the IRS is requiring Mary to take. In fact, it's over 30 percent more than what Morningstar's experts consider

---

8   Blanchett, Finke, and Pfau, "Low Bond Yields," Morningstar.

"safe" if the goal is to be highly certain you won't run out of money in retirement.

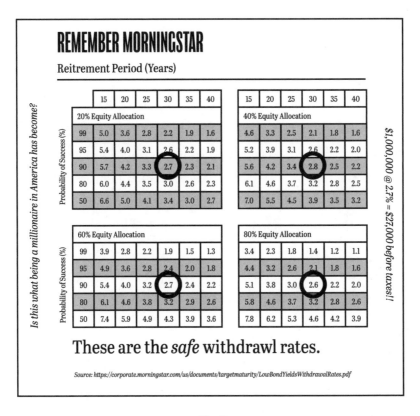

Fig. 8

Here is the withdrawal grid that describes the safe withdrawal rate based on retirement period and asset allocation. This grid from the Morningstar study defines your probability of success based on your account not going to zero. In other words, it defines success as your ability to climb back down the mountain after scaling the top. Success, in this report, does not mean that your basis (the principal, invested capital) in your account is preserved but that your account will not run down to a $0 balance before you die.

That is the definition of success in this academic paper written by experts in economics and finance. Again, they don't define success as mass accumulation of funds; they define it as the ability to maintain a balance greater than zero in your account, despite taking annual distributions at various rates.

There's even more that we can take away from this Morningstar report: the impact our various investments have on our safe withdrawal rates. Looking at the chart, you'll see that there are a few different situations taken into consideration. In one column, it says *20 percent equity allocation.* In the next quadrant over, it says *40 percent equity allocation,* then 60 percent below, and then 80 percent in the far-right lower quadrant. What this is telling you is that the most you can take out of an account that's 20 percent invested in the stock market is 2.7 percent. That limit will give you 90 percent certainty that you aren't going to run out of money.

If you have 40 percent of your money invested in stocks or stock funds, Morningstar discovered that you could confidently take out 2.8 percent per year. So accumulation is good, right? The more risk you take, the more you accumulate and the higher your income could potentially be! Except, that's not true when your objective is to receive retirement income. Look at the quadrant for those with 60 percent of their assets in the market. Their distribution rate has fallen back down to 2.7 percent. Those with 80 percent of their assets in the market are kicked back down to 2.6 percent withdrawals—and on top of that, this added risk increases your chances of losing your basis, or your principal investment, in a volatile market. Exceed these numbers and you are significantly increasing your mathematical risk of going broke in retirement.

When you think about it, if the required minimum distribution rate in year one for a healthy, vigorous 70.5-year-old is roughly 3.649

percent, and if we consider the stock and bond market as one huge portfolio, with roughly ten thousand baby boomers turning 70.5 years old each day, we start to see that this is creating a tremendous amount of cash-flow pressure, and that pressure is building—and it's only going to get worse. Let me show you why.

REQUIRED MINIMUM DISTRIBUTION

Table III (Uniform Lifetime)

Age	Distribution Period	Age	Distribution Period	Age	Distribution Period	Age	Distribution Period
70	27.4	82	17.1	94	9.1	106	4.2
71	26.5	83	16.3	95	8.6	107	3.9
72	25.6	84	15.5	96	8.1	108	3.7
73	24.7	85	14.8	97	7.6	109	3.4
74	23.8	86	14.1	98	7.1	110	3.1
75	22.9	87	13.4	99	6.7	111	2.9
76	22.0	88	12.7	100	6.3	112	2.6
77	21.2	89	12.0	101	5.9	113	2.4
78	20.3	90	11.4	102	5.5	114	2.1
79	19.5	91	10.8	103	5.2	115 and over	1.9
80	18.7	92	10.2	104	4.9		
81	17.9	93	9.6	105	4.5		

Once you determine a separate required minimum distribution from each of your traditional IRAs, you can total these minimum amounts and take them from any one or more of your traditional IRAs.

Fig. 9

By age eighty, the divisor for the minimum distribution goes down (from 27.4 at 70.5, to 18.7 at age eighty). This means that the required amount of distributions from your IRA and 401(k) account goes up. Let's see what that does to our required minimum distribution.

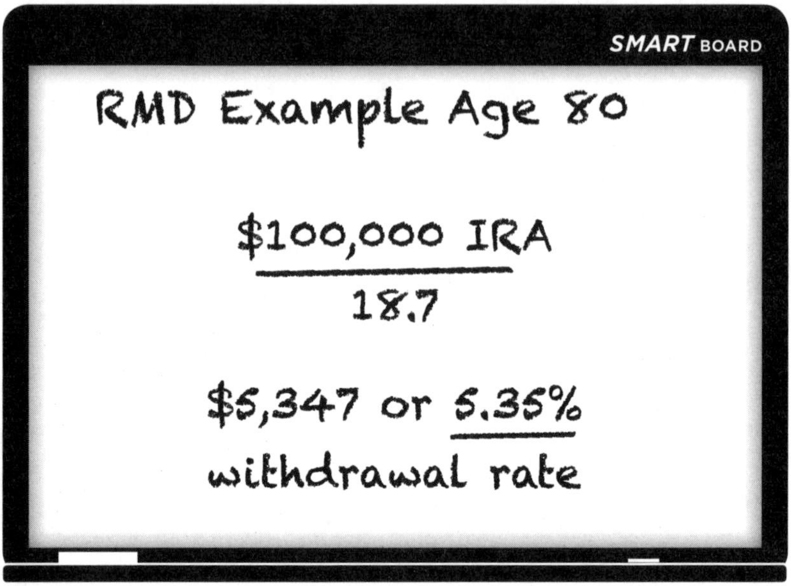

Fig. 10

If we take that same $100,000 and consider that our client is now eighty years old and we do that division, then that means that the required minimum distribution now is $5,347 or 5.35 percent as a distribution rate—almost twice as much as Morningstar suggests is advisable to avoid hitting a $0 balance. I believe that's an unsustainable amount of pressure on the market as ten thousand or so new retirees turn 70.5 years old every day and another ten thousand or so turn eighty years old every day. Still, you might think that's going to slow down eventually—it's not going to be ten thousand boomers turning sixty-five years old every day forever. And while that's true, with advancements in medical technology, more and more retirees are living healthy and productive lives into their eighties and nineties, which means we're going to carry the burden of the boomers for a very long time.

But the great salvation, say Wall Street and the economists they pay to agree, is that the millennials are coming to the party. But guess what they're strapped with? Student loan debts totaling more than $1 trillion![9] They're not even funding their own retirement plans like 401(k)s that invest in the stock and bond markets, because they have these large debts to pay that they've accumulated getting their education. But it's not just the debt—it's also that millennials actively distrust the stock market. A 2015 poll conducted by Bloomberg found that almost 40 percent of millennial respondents did not trust the stock market, often citing that it is too volatile or that it wasn't fair for small investors.[10] The Great Recession of 2008 permanently scarred their young minds, as they heard countless financial horror stories from their parents and relatives who lost half their retirement money to a crashing stock market. It was essentially the millennials' equivalent to the Great Depression. All of this, in turn, leads us to this: the complete failure of traditional financial planning models at every age and in every way.

Inflation is something that's going to hurt us all. The budget you make now for your planned retirement spending is fine, except for just one thing: you don't have any idea how much everything will actually cost once you retire. On average, we can expect inflation to raise

---

9   Libby Kane, "Student Loan Debt in the US Has Topped $1.3 Trillion," *Business Insider*, January 12, 2016, www.businessinsider.com/student-loan-debt-state-of-the-union-2016-1.

10   Callie Bost, "Millennials Don't Trust Stock Market, Goldman Sachs Poll Shows," *Bloomberg*, June 24, 2015, www.bloomberg.com/news/articles/2015-06-24/millennials-don-t-trust-the-stock-market-says-goldman-sachs-poll.

the cost of goods and services by 3.22 percent a year. But, like fluctuating returns, inflation rates vary, such as in 1990 when inflation averaged 5.4 percent or in 1974 when inflation averaged 11 percent.[11] Should you retire during or after a period of excessive inflation, you might deplete your savings far quicker than you expected, unless you have a plan to preserve your savings from the equally damaging impact of taxes.

It's also worth considering the fact that inflation is a multidimensional thing. It's not just an increase in prices. Most Americans would agree that their view of inflation has to do with the prices of certain items and if the prices of those items they buy most frequently are up from the prior year, then they know they are dealing with the effects of inflation.

But the other concern we need to think about is monetary inflation, which is a whole different type of inflation. It is a simple inflation to track because it simply means the government is asking the Federal Reserve to print more money. They are asking to inflate the amount of money available. Modern monetary inflation started during the Kennedy administration and has been a steady policy in Washington since it began, regardless of political party. Democrats have inflated money supply just as the Republicans have inflated the money supply. And you know what? We, as Americans, like it. More money around equals the feeling of greater prosperity . . . as long as the money holds its value, and with close to $4 trillion

---

[11]   Bureau of Labor Statistics, "CPI Inflation Calculator," https://www.bls.gov/data/inflation_calculator.htm.

added to the money supply since 2008, it's very possible that it won't.[12]

Monetary inflation played a key role in the decision to abandon the gold standard in the US, on August 15, 1971, leading to the "Nixon Shock." In essence, the change to a floating exchange rate in the US represented a form of reset for our own currency right here in the United States.

Price inflation hurts us most while in retirement because most retirees live off a fixed income, so it is especially painful if the interest rates available from safe investments and bank-offered savings plans are low. It is a classic case of "costs are up and revenue is flat." However, there is a lot more to it once you also factor in the dangers of monetary inflation. We each need to ask ourselves and our advisors what's being done with our finances to manage that possibility? One of the best moves we can make is to preserve more of our assets and keep them safe from taxation.

---

12   Mike Patton, "Why Inflation Is Low, Despite the Fed's Massive Monetary Expansion," Forbes, December 28, 2015, http://www.forbes.com/sites/mikepatton/2015/12/28/why-inflation-is-low-despite-the-feds-massive-monetary-expansion/.

CHAPTER 2

THE TRUTH ABOUT THE MISLEADING FINANCIAL MATH BANKS AND WALL STREET USE

Resulting in the Epic Failure of Traditional Financial Planning and Investment Advice to Protect Us from Their "Fuzzy" Math

It's hard to swallow the truth about traditional planning's failure and misleading math from banks and Wall Street brokerage firms, but I believe you can handle it. More than that, you must be aware of the truth and you must dig into the realities of finance so that you don't become a victim of the purposefully meaningless mathematical formulas put forth by the banks and the brokerage community.

Earlier, I mentioned student loan debt. Let's dig deeper into that. Right now, the average borrower in the college graduating class of

2014 carries more than $33,000 in student loan debt.[13] Many of them don't realize how toxic this debt is to their future wealth accumulation and retirement, especially since much of it was issued with such low interest rates—but are low interest rates *really* that low? The answer is no. Because in truth, interest rates are a big part of the tricky mathematical formulas put out by banks and the Wall Street brokerage and investment community—a simple math trick that creates incredible wealth for banks and bankers. Don't believe me? See for yourself:

Amount	$100,000
Term	30 yr. 0 mo.
Rate	4.0%

What's the interest rate? 4 percent?

Are you *sure* it's 4 percent?

Fig. 11

Let's say that you're very proud of your young grandson who is going to buy his first house for $100,000 with a thirty-year mortgage at a 4 percent interest rate. He scored this low rate because he's a hardworking guy with good credit. While you're telling your friends about his financial acumen, you mention his interest rate: 4 percent. You know that's his rate because it says so on all his documents, right? But there are a couple of things wrong with that. Something doesn't quite add up.

---

13   "Students & Debt," debt.org/students.

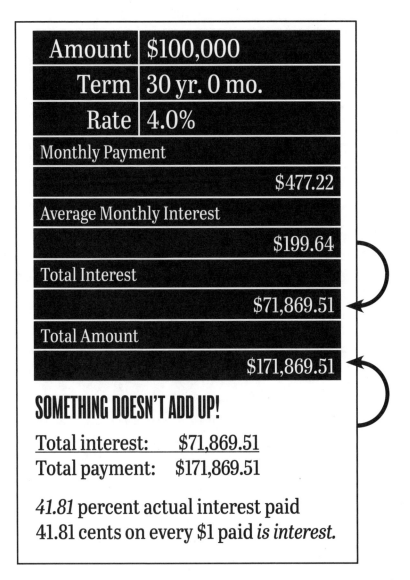

Amount	$100,000
Term	30 yr. 0 mo.
Rate	4.0%

Monthly Payment	
	$477.22

Average Monthly Interest	
	$199.64

Total Interest	
	$71,869.51

Total Amount	
	$171,869.51

SOMETHING DOESN'T ADD UP!

Total interest: $71,869.51

Total payment: $171,869.51

41.81 percent actual interest paid

41.81 cents on every $1 paid *is interest.*

Fig. 12

If we look at the total interest your grandson is going to pay on this loan and we divide that by the total payments he makes, it's going to tell a different story. You see the word *rate* is really a mathematical function of speed. It's like when you go to your doctor and one of the nurses there, Janet, gives you a shot and, zoom, she really shoots that volume of medicine into you very quickly. In this instance, her rate is high, very fast. It's a quotient of speed. But then you have another nurse, Mary, who puts that shot into your arm and very slowly injects the medication. It's the same amount of medication, but it takes a lot longer this time around. That is what rate is all about, the speed. Yet, what really matters isn't the speed but the *volume* of medicine you get. The right amount will help you get better, but too much and you're dead. Volume is also what matters when you look at the interest you pay. It's really about the total amount of interest out of your pocket—not the speed at which you're paying it.

When we look at volume of interest we need to look at something a little different than just the rate. We need to look at the total amount of interest paid. In the case of your hypothetical grandson, a $100,000 mortgage over thirty years at a 4 percent interest rate equals $71,869.51 in interest over the full term of the loan. Not the $4,000 you'd expect if you multiplied $100,000 by 4 percent. Add that interest amount to the $100,000 that your grandson borrowed and the total amount of payments is $171,869.51. So what is the actual percentage of interest paid on every dollar? A horrifying 41.81 percent. That's how I want to look at it. If I'm paying a dollar, how much is going to interest? Well, it's actually 41.81 cents of every dollar paid going to satisfy the interest payments. And this actually is a best-case scenario, because most people don't keep a thirty-year mortgage for thirty years. If you're familiar with how amortization works, you'll know that there's more interest paid in the early years. So if you refinance every seven to nine years, these interest rates can easily double to more than 60 percent.

Another detrimental choice being foisted on today's society is leasing. Leasing is a way for dealers to get younger folks to basically agree to a lifetime payment in exchange for never owning a thing. It's incalculable how much interest is being paid on leases, because we never truly own the asset.

Bankers use these sneaky tricks to ensure that consumers don't fully see the impact of debt. This process also makes it almost impossible for consumers to get free from the cycle of debt without extreme cost. In turn, this reduces their savings power and their overall wealth potential, which I refer to as Lifetime Economic Earnings Velocity, making retirement planning that much more difficult.

We all know that the earlier we start saving, the more money we will eventually have. Look at this chart:

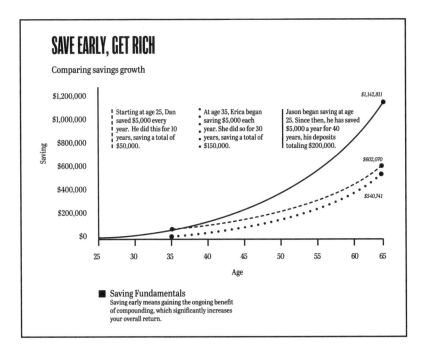

SAVE EARLY, GET RICH

Comparing savings growth

Starting at age 25, Dan saved $5,000 every year. He did this for 10 years, saving a total of $50,000.

At age 35, Erica began saving $5,000 each year. She did so for 30 years, saving a total of $150,000.

Jason began saving at age 25. Since then, he has saved $5,000 a year for 40 years, his deposits totaling $200,000.

$1,142,811

$602,070

$540,741

■ Saving Fundamentals
Saving early means gaining the ongoing benefit of compounding, which significantly increases your overall return.

Fig. 13

In reviewing this chart, you realize that the mantra we should all live by is: Start Early, Get Rich! But the banks make that hard to do when people face actual interest rates and a true volume of interest between 20 and 60 percent.

Losing lifetime economic earnings velocity isn't just a problem faced by young people. Retirees and preretirees are also victims, with many of them in a race to pay off their house or car, only to find themselves dragging the even-more-harmful credit card debt into retirement. Often, the solution is a combination of debt consolidation and simply forced savings into tax-exempt assets.

Recently we worked with a client who was carrying a mortgage, home equity line of credit and over $20,000 of credit card debt with only five years left before his desired retirement age.

By using our *Debt Elimination Before Retirement* process he was on the path to being paid off on time for his retirement but with an extra $54,000 of cash in his pocket plus a decent amount of paid-up life insurance that he could rely on to take care of his wife and family later on.

So many retirees and preretirees don't realize that finding the right approach to debt elimination is just as important as funding their 401(k). They mismanage their cash flow and debts—often trying to target a pay-off date without factoring in or even understanding how the volume of interest really works. The trick is to understand the truth about debt math —something your local bank, which benefits from all the interest you pay, certainly won't share with you.

At the same time, we have a different mathematical trick being played on us by the folks on Wall Street, and it's called *rate of return*. They've convinced us that all that really matters is how much rate of return we're earning.

Now, rate of return has got some validity to it, but it's only half the story. If I said to you, "Hey, look, there's a mountain. Let's go climb it," would our objective be just to get to the top of the mountain, or would it be to get to the top of the mountain, take our pictures, and get back down safely so we can go home? Naturally, no one wants to plan only to climb the mountain—they want to also plan to get back down again. Retirement planning, believe it or not, is a lot like climbing a mountain. In preretirement, your accumulation and rate of return are significant. They represent your climb up the mountain. But as you'll soon learn, in the distribution phase—that time when you're actually in retirement and you're getting income from your assets—the math changes significantly.

What if I told you I had this amazing crystal ball that was never wrong and I proved it to you? I say, "Your Aunt May is going to call you right now," and the phone rings and sure enough, it is Aunt May. Then I say your cousin will win the lottery tomorrow, and she does. Then we do a few more things like this until you have complete faith in the crystal ball. If after proving all that to you, I tell you that I was looking in the crystal ball and I saw that the stock market is going to earn an average of 14.84 percent over the next thirty years, you'd be excited, right? Why wouldn't you be? I'd be excited, too. Let's check this retirement out and talk about how well that crystal ball did for us.

THE DANGERS OF AN AVERAGE RATE OF RETURN

Beginning retirement asset value = $1,000,000   10% of beginning value = ($100,000)

Number of years = 30   Average return = 14.84%

Constant Returns

Retirement Year	Annual Return	Annual Income	Account Value
1	14.84%	-$100,000	$1,033,290
2	14.84%	-$100,000	$1,072,100
3	14.84%	-$100,000	$1,116,360
4	14.84%	-$100,000	$1,167,188
5	14.84%	-$100,000	$1,225,558
6	14.84%	-$100,000	$1,292,591
7	14.84%	-$100,000	$1,369,572
8	14.84%	-$100,000	$1,457,976
9	14.84%	-$100,000	$1,559,500
10	14.84%	-$100,000	$1,676,090
11	14.84%	-$100,000	$1,809,982
12	14.84%	-$100,000	$1,963,743
13	14.84%	-$100,000	$2,140,322
14	14.84%	-$100,000	$2,343,106
15	14.84%	-$100,000	$2,575,983
20	14.84%	-$100,000	$4,373,434
25	14.84%	-$100,000	$7,963,668
30	14.84%	-$100,000	$15,134,818

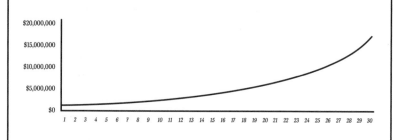

Fig. 14

Thanks to the crystal ball, you're going to take $1 million and we'll have a constant rate of return of 14.84 percent and, being the conservative adult you are, you decide to just take $100,000 out every year. After ten years, you will have taken out $1 million of income and you'd still have $1.676 million in your account. Not only did you get to enjoy $1 million of income and the retirement lifestyle it buys, but you also grew your wealth by more than $676,000. After twenty years, it gets even better. You've taken out $2 million, but that little bit extra that you've left behind has compounded, all the way to $4.3 million. What a plan, right? After thirty years, your family's around you in your giant mansion, you've taken $3 million of income out, and you're leaving a massive amount of wealth—to the tune of $15.134 million—to your loved ones. Three million dollars in income and $15 million to the family—all because the crystal ball was never wrong.

But maybe we're jumping to conclusions here without analyzing all the facts. Because the crystal ball never told us *how* that 14.84 percent was actually earned. It just said over the next thirty years the market is going to *average* 14.84 percent. Now, if we were in the accumulation phase for thirty years, that would be great. But if we're in the distribution phase—climbing down that mountain after saving for retirement—then the actual numbers look quite different. Let's take a look at the real numbers and see what happens if we actually tried to implement the plan.

CONSTANT VS. FLUCTUATING RETURNS

Range of years   =   1970-1999   *Average* return   =   14.84%

History of the S&P 500

Year	Annual Return	Year	Annual Return
1970	3.99%	1985	31.65%
1971	14.33%	1986	18.60%
1972	18.94%	1987	5.17%
1973	-14.79%	1988	16.61%
1974	-26.54%	1989	31.69%
1975	37.25%	1990	-3.10%
1976	23.67%	1991	30.47%
1977	-7.39%	1992	7.62%
1978	6.44%	1993	10.08%
1979	18.35%	1994	1.32%
1980	32.27%	1995	37.58%
1981	-5.05%	1996	22.96%
1982	21.48%	1997	33.36%
1983	22.50%	1998	28.58%
1984	6.15%	1999	21.04%

Fig. 15

First off, you notice that the word *average* is italicized? That's because the stock market doesn't offer us a static, fixed return—it offers us a fluctuating return. The crystal ball was definitely correct, but once you begin taking income, rate of return is no longer the focal point. Something new matters, and that's called *sequence of returns.*

When you have variable investments in your retirement accounts, such as bonds, mutual funds, ETFs, and stocks, their returns fluctuate based on a variety of reasons far outside your control, such as perceived value, demand, news events, and more. If you have low or no returns in the early years and you maintain normal distributions, then you deplete your capital before it has had a chance to replenish itself. By the time the higher returns happen, you have already drained the account by so much that there is not enough left in it to grow sufficiently to help you maintain that lifetime income or your principal balance—which means you lose *both*.

This, essentially, is the problem with sequence of returns risk.

THE REAL RISK: SEQUENCE OF RETURNS

Beginning retirement asset value	= $1,000,000	10% of beginning value	= ($100,000)
Number of years	= 30	Average return	= 14.84%

Fluctuating Returns

Year	Annual Return	Annual Income	Account Value
1	3.99%	-$100,000	$935,910
2	14.33%	-$100,000	$955,696
3	18.94%	-$100,000	$1,017,765
4	-14.79%	-$100,000	$782,027
5	-26.54%	-$100,000	$501,017
6	37.25%	-$100,000	$550,396
7	23.67%	-$100,000	$557,005
8	-7.39%	-$100,000	$423,232
9	6.44%	-$100,000	$344,048
10	18.35%	-$100,000	$288,831
11	32.27%	-$100,000	$249,767
12	-5.05%	-$100,000	$142,204
13	21.48%	-$100,000	$51,269
14	22.50%	-$51,269	$0
15	6.15%	$0	$0

Fig. 16

Let's try to implement our plan now with a fluctuating rate of return. In year 1, you're down quite a bit. So you call the advisor and say, "Hey, I've got my $100,000 income this year, but I'm down to $935,000 here. I'm a little bit nervous." The advisor tells you not to worry, it will come back, it's just that kind of year. And because you saw that crystal ball, which you know to be accurate, you believe the advisor. The next year you take another $100,000 out, so you have now had $200,000 of retirement income taken from this account, and your balance does go up to $955,000. You think, *This is headed in the right direction; it's actually working out.* In year 3, you take another $100,000 and your balance shoots up to over $1 million. Now you're at the country club and you're with your friends and you're telling them how amazing your financial advisor is. You brag to your golfing buddies that you've taken out $300,000 over the past three years, yet you're actually at a gain on your $1 million investment. They look at you in awe, thinking they must go see your advisor, right?

Well, year 4 comes around. It's 1973 and, bam, you're down 14 percent. You take $100,000 out, as usual, and at the end of the year your balance is $782,027. You call your advisor and say, "Whoa, I'm really nervous here." Your advisor says, "Hey, remember what happened last time? This is just a bigger correction. You need to hold on and it's going to come back." But that's not what happens. Instead, year 5 rolls around and you take out your next $100,000 and the market tanks another 26 percent—and your balance is down to $500,000 and, from your perspective, you've lost half of your money.

Now for the vast majority of us that's the "uncle" point. We're done and we cry "Uncle!" We are going to take that money out, put it in a CD, and live a very meager existence in retirement because of the tremendous amount of wealth that we've just lost. But if you're stubborn—I had one uncle who was stubborn as a mule; he'd have probably said, "I'm just going to keep getting my $100,000 out. It's supposed to work, the crystal ball said so," and he would keep taking it. If you were stubborn like that, you would see that by year 13 you have lost all your money. This really illustrates the significant difference that rate of return plays when considering accumulation and distribution. If the sequence of returns is poor, then you have the very real possibility of losing all of your money. When you need that retirement income, or are required to take income (RMDs) from your retirement accounts, if you want to keep your money intact, then you have to be smarter about how you approach your distributions in the future.

In a 2016 *Forbes* article, Wade Pfau, professor of retirement income at the American College, wrote, "Taking distributions from an investment portfolio amplifies the impact of portfolio volatility, making retirement income planning particularly tricky, as distributions tend to be the primary income source for retirees."[14] In the good years, when the market never seems to stop climbing, the idea of performance being amplified sounds pretty good. But in the bad years, like in 2008, when the bottom just seems to fall out of the financial world, amplified volatility can spell disaster for retirees who have no time—or income—to reinvest and eventually recover from losses.

---

14   Wade Pfau, "Weighing Sequence of Returns Risk For Retirees," *Forbes*, August 2, 2016, www.forbes.com/sites/wadepfau/2016/08/02/weighing-sequence-of-returns-risk-for-retirees /#6875d830f242.

In 2016, when talking about sequence of returns risk in another article, Pfau wrote, "The financial market returns experienced near retirement matter a great deal more than most people realize. Even with the same average returns over a long period of time, retiring at the start of a bear market is very dangerous; wealth can be rapidly depleted as withdrawals are made from a diminishing portfolio, leaving little money to benefit from a subsequent market recovery."[15] Yet, how can a retiree plan to retire and begin taking distributions at the right time? A time when the market is rising—not losing? Frankly, they can't. Instead, they need to focus on what they *can* control, namely how much they pay in taxes and where they take their income from.

We have to remember, too, that Morningstar is telling us it doesn't really matter if we're 20 percent, 40 percent, 60 percent, or even 80 percent in the stock market, the amount we can withdraw is relatively similar, falling somewhere between 2.6 and 2.8 percent. When we were new in the business, the industry powers-that-be taught us advisors that everything was about our asset allocation. Heck, the creators of the concept of asset allocation won a Nobel Prize in 1990.[16] But we've since learned from experience that this isn't true. Is this what being a millionaire in America has become? Taking 2.7 percent on $1 million is $27,000. And if it's in a traditional IRA or 401(k) account, then that's *before* taxes. How are we going to make ends meet if we believe taxes are going up? How do we make ends

15   Wade Pfau, "Navigating One of The Greatest Risks Of Retirement Income Planning," *Forbes*, June 20, 2016, www.forbes.com/sites/wadepfau/2016/06/20/navigating-one-of-the-greatest-risks-of-retirement-income-planning/#5b7fac575fc1.
16   "This Year's Laureates are Pioneers in the Theory of Financial Economics and Corporate Finance," October 16, 1990, www.nobelprize.org/nobel_prizes/economic-sciences/laureates/1990/press.html.

meet if we believe that health insurance is going to become exponentially more expensive? How are we going to make our money last if we believe that taxes are going to go up *and* health insurance is going to get more expensive?

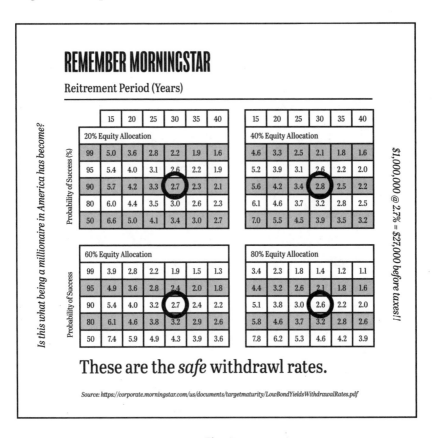

Fig. 17

Obviously, we can't make these low retirement income distribution rates work, and on top of it we have to be smart about how big a role we allow taxes to play in our net income—because in that, we are not powerless. Our future taxes are a direct result of the choices we make now. In fact, all the financial decisions you make now have a compound effect on your future liabilities. That's why we need to work on the Strategic Movement Around Retirement Taxation®—in order to have the *right* compound effect and control our future tax liabilities. Because the tax code's pretty clear: you have to pay tax once. Yet many of the decisions made by people today (based on the advice of their advisors) make them pay taxes over and over and over again.

After seeing the difference in returns between a fixed-rate product and one that fluctuates, you might be wondering where you can get a fixed product with that impressive a return. The truth is, you can't. The good news is, you really don't need to. Think about it this way, a return could be substantially lower than the 14.84 percent used in the example and it would still help you maintain an ongoing balance of $1 million while taking income distributions of $50,000 to $80,000 per year (depending on your age and prevailing interest rates). There is no need to risk it all to try to grow your account to $15 million in thirty years when your goal, really, is to receive a comfortable, continual income stream, which is what most people want out of their personal retirement plan.

Fixed products, such as bonds and money market accounts, typically have lower returns than other investments because they are lower in risk and some are guaranteed—something no stock offers. But that lowered risk helps to ensure that you can get a return of your capital. There's even more good news, though: when you're retired, you're living off of the withdrawal rate, not the rate of return you've gotten. So it's more important to find ways to guarantee the safety of your capital and ensure its return than it is to find a high yield. Why? In part because a higher yield means more fluctuation and, as we discussed, that can completely wipe you out. But that's not all. There are ways to plan around a lower return so that your withdrawals are more effective through actuarial arbitrage (like float) and are tax efficient, which we'll discuss in more detail in the next chapter.

WALL STREET WIZARDRY

Did you know that a dollar you get today is worth more than a dollar you get tomorrow? It's true. A concept called the *time value of money* teaches us that a dollar you receive today has time to earn interest and compound and has more spending power than it will in a year when inflation has raised the costs of goods and services. This concept helps us understand why it's so important that you manage your eventual tax liabilities and that you truly understand what you're getting—or not getting—in terms of returns.

To illustrate how returns can be misleading, I want to do some Wall Street wizardry. To do this, let's do some simple math.

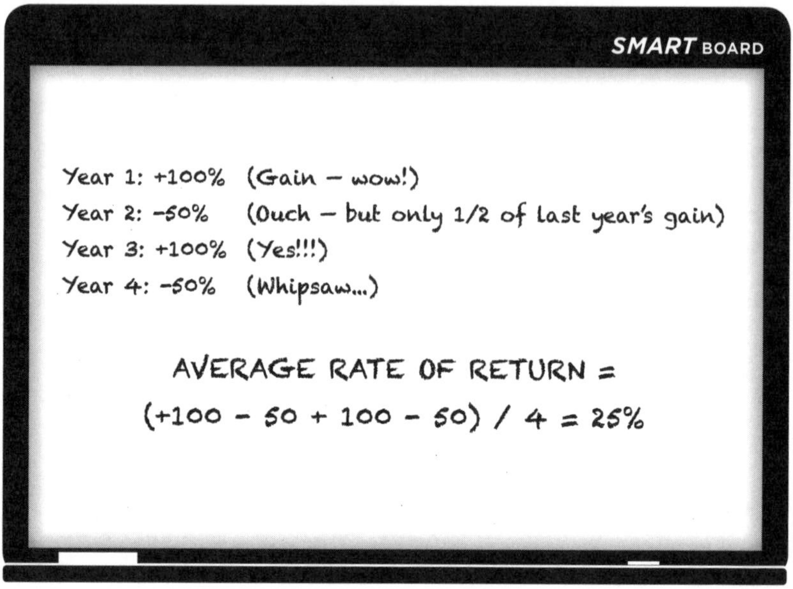
SMART BOARD
Year 1: +100% (Gain – wow!)
Year 2: -50% (Ouch – but only 1/2 of last year's gain)
Year 3: +100% (Yes!!!)
Year 4: -50% (Whipsaw...)
AVERAGE RATE OF RETURN =
(+100 - 50 + 100 - 50) / 4 = 25%

Fig. 18

An average return of 25 percent is nothing to complain about, and it certainly helps to improve the value of your money in the future. Now let's see how this looks when we turn this hypothetical return into a real example with $10,000.

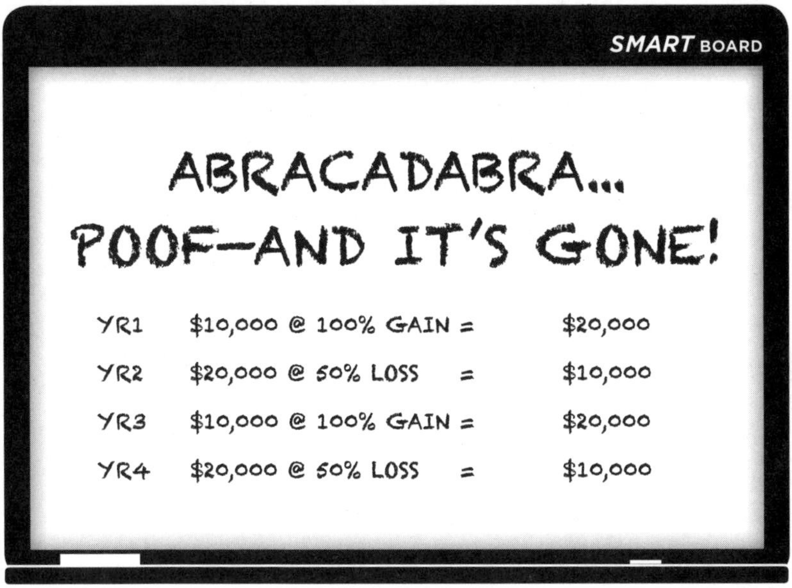

SMART BOARD

ABRACADABRA...
POOF—AND IT'S GONE!

YR1	$10,000 @ 100% GAIN =	$20,000
YR2	$20,000 @ 50% LOSS =	$10,000
YR3	$10,000 @ 100% GAIN =	$20,000
YR4	$20,000 @ 50% LOSS =	$10,000

Fig. 19

While it's true that the average rate of return was 25 percent, it's also true that you got zero growth on your $10,000 investment. Beware of Wall Street math wizardry!

PLANNING YOUR DESCENT: MORE IMPORTANT THAN THE CLIMB

I can't imagine anyone looking forward to being stranded at the top of a mountain they just worked so hard to climb. I also can't imagine any retiree working hard to save and preserve money during their working years just so they can pay much of it out in taxes just a few years after retirement and be left stranded, relying primarily on Social Security to get them through.

There are many challenges facing us as we work to create a lasting, tax-efficient retirement plan, but there are ways to still accomplish this despite the challenges. In the next chapter, I introduce you to the SMART retirement plan—an optimal way to strategically move around retirement taxation so that you can enjoy greater, ongoing financial independence and gain comfortable peace of mind.

It's time to learn a smarter and better way.

CHAPTER 3

USING BASIS AND FLOAT TO GAIN FINANCIAL FREEDOM

Let's talk about what it means to have a SMART retirement. To us, SMART means ensuring that your money makes a Strategic Movement Around Retirement Taxation®. The goal here is to maximize your after-tax retirement income over what conventional traditional financial planning can provide, while targeting a 0 percent tax rate (when possible) in your retirement. Now, this is not always possible, but it makes sense that we should target as low a tax bracket as we possibly can so that the majority of your retirement income is spendable.

You've no doubt noticed that today, everyone has smartphones and smart TVs. But what about smart money? What can we do to make the money that we have smarter? How can we make it work better and have more functionality in our future retirement years?

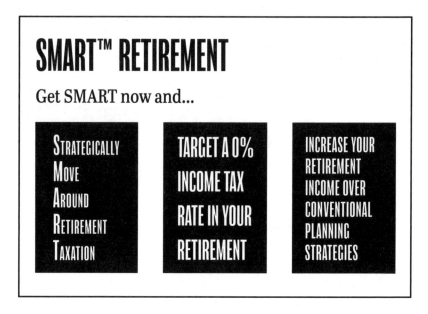

Fig. 20

ALL ABOUT THAT BASIS

Will Rogers is credited as having said, "I am not so much concerned with the return *on* my capital as I am with the return *of* my capital." This is a quote that really highlights what I think has been lost along the way, especially by 401(k) advisors, and that is that the word *basis* means a lot. If we were a bunch of accountants reading this, we would all know exactly what *basis* means. Since we're not, let me explain. Basis is the amount of capital we've actually paid in. It is the total amount we have put into each investment—it's our outlay *of* capital. It's funny how frequently I run into somebody who has a 401(k) plan, and when I ask them how much they've invested into their 401(k) account, they want to tell me a percentage and how much the company matches. But I say, "No, no, no. How much money have you contributed in dollar form?" And almost nobody ever has an answer to that question. In order to create a SMART plan, we really need to understand what our basis paid in is and how to make our money work beyond that basis.

Of course, knowing how much you've contributed doesn't, in and of itself, ensure that you will get all of it back or manage its growth well. But what it does is ensure is that you can create a plan to secure all the capital you've contributed. A way to neutralize losses and make sure the full amount of your capital remains accessible to you in retirement.

A few decades ago, this wasn't as important. Back then, most employers, even those in the private sector, had pension plans set up for employees. Pension plans are also called *defined benefit* plans because they are established with the purpose of paying out a set monthly payment to retirees. Because retirees could count on those payments, and because they were fully funded by the employer— with absolutely no money paid in by the employees—there was no need to be concerned about the basis. Likewise, there was no need to be concerned about future retirement income. The pension plan was funded for you, based on your salary and years of service. It was a simple plan that put all of the investment risk and responsibility on the employer.

Now things have changed. Employers have embraced a different model for retirement planning—the *defined contribution* plan. In this model, the employee contributes a certain amount of their pay and the company may or may not match a portion of it. Worse, you have to make all the investment decisions, and losses in the account are losses of *your money*—and your potential future income. There is no guaranteed payout for the retiree to count on. That means it's absolutely crucial to understand what you've invested in and exactly how much your basis is—to define how much you've contributed, if you will—so that you can make sure that amount is working for you and, as Will Rogers advises, it will eventually be returned to you in the form of retirement income, we hope with significant gains.

I want to return to the word *float*. If you've ever read anything about Warren Buffett, the most successful investor in the entire country, then you may know that profiting from insurance float is something that he has focused Berkshire Hathaway on. We can be like Buffett, too, and profit from understanding how actuaries price different types of insurance products so that we can get a greater return, significantly reduce risk, and achieve a lower tax liability.

Warren Buffett, owner of the holding company Berkshire Hathaway, is our country's most successful and celebrated investor. As you can imagine, it takes a certain amount of insight, courage, and knowledge to reach the heights of success that he has. One of the ways he's been so successful is by shunning conventionally accepted interpretations of investing and accounting and, instead, looking at the math of a situation and capitalizing on the story it tells. This is how Buffett was able to recognize and use the profit potential of *float*. And he doesn't keep all this to himself. He is so impressed with the way float has helped him grow his wealth that he mentions the term forty-six times in his 2015 letter to Berkshire Hathaway shareholders. And that's not the first time he's mentioned it. Here's what he said about float in his 2014 letter:

So how does our float affect intrinsic value? When Berkshire's *book* value is calculated, the *full* amount of our float is deducted as a *liability*, just as if we had to pay it out tomorrow and could not replenish it. But to think of float as strictly a liability is incorrect; it should instead be viewed as a revolving fund.[17]

You and I may not be on Warren Buffett's level, but we can still try to understand float and use it in our own SMART plans. And believe me when I tell you—it's worth it. Float is, essentially, the money an insurance company has in reserve to pay out future claims. You see, insurance companies routinely collect premiums, yet they don't always pay these premiums out in claims immediately since most claims are made far into the future. To capitalize on the time lag between the date they collect premiums and the far future date they have to pay those premiums back out as claims, insurance companies invest the premium dollars and earn interest, at least until they have to pay them back out for claims. So, as Buffett tells us, accountants have to look at that float as a liability since it may eventually be paid out in claims, but for him—and for us—it's possible to continue to collect interest on that money. Because of this, Buffett believes the market is undervaluing his huge company since it doesn't understand, under current accounting rules, the true value of his company's float as an asset.

---

17   "2014 Annual Report," Berkshire Hathaway, Inc., www.berkshirehathaway.com/2014ar/2014ar.pdf.

SMART is a two-pronged approach to successful retirement planning. When people ask me what I do, I tell them I am best known for the work I've done with tax and actuarial arbitrage for my clients. Now *arbitrage* is a big, fancy word but all it means is that we're going to take a profitable advantage of differences. Like, imagine buying a used car for $500 from a seller who's desperate to get rid of it and at the same time having a signed agreement in hand to sell it to an eager buyer with a cashier's check for $700. That's arbitrage.

That's what we're going to focus on, how to take a profitable advantage of differences in tax rates using low- to no-risk, insurance-based products in a complementary way that's different than the way that these products are traditionally marketed to the public.

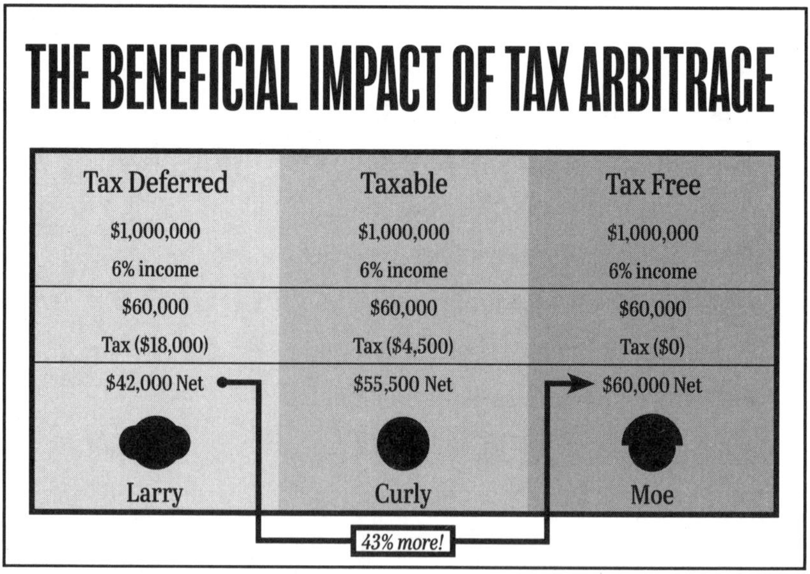

THE BENEFICIAL IMPACT OF TAX ARBITRAGE

Tax Deferred	Taxable	Tax Free
$1,000,000	$1,000,000	$1,000,000
6% income	6% income	6% income
$60,000	$60,000	$60,000
Tax ($18,000)	Tax ($4,500)	Tax ($0)
$42,000 Net	$55,500 Net	$60,000 Net
Larry	Curly	Moe

43% more!

Fig. 21

Let's get into the nitty-gritty of tax arbitrage by using the Three Stooges as an example. Say hello to Larry, Curly, and Moe.

Larry was always the smart one. His accountant told him to put his money away in a tax-deferred plan, so he did. His advisor helped him to grow his money well, so he wasn't too worried about his future retirement. At retirement, based on current interest rates, he was able to take 6 percent out. Of course, he didn't know what his tax rate would be at that point. But he was told, as so many are, that he would be in a lower tax bracket in his senior years, and he trusted that information.

Curly liked stocks, so he invested in the stock market and kept track of his cost basis. He put money into a regular old taxable account and when he took the money out he knew he would have to pay capital gains on the growth. Like Larry, Curly knew he could take out around 6 percent because that was the prevailing interest rate at the time.

Moe, on the other hand, was always a little more conservative. He was worried he'd make a "dumb" investment, so he put his money into a safe, simple savings-type vehicle through an insurance company, which allowed him to take tax-free distributions of 6 percent (the prevailing rate) once he retired. Even though he had to put in more money to make up for the slower growth rate, he knew he wouldn't have to deal with the unpredictability of the market and taxes. Now let's see how this worked out:

- It looks like Larry, with his tax-deferred savings, got the shortest end of the stick. Taking out $60,000 gross income and being forced to pay ordinary income taxes on that income leaves him with just $42,000 to spend each year.

- Curly faired better *with a taxable account* because he'd already locked in his basis earlier along with lower capital gains tax rate and now simply has to pay on his gains, leaving him with $55,500 to spend each year.

- But it's Moe who really found the best way to plan his retirement. For him, there is no tax on the $60,000 annual withdrawal, leaving him with the full $60,000 to spend each year—43 percent more income than Larry.

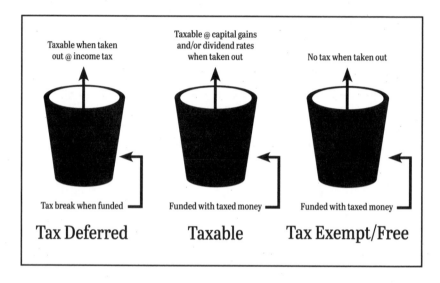

Fig. 22

Take a look at Figure 22 and imagine that you could take your retirement income from any one of these three buckets. Which would you choose? Would you choose the tax-deferred bucket, which guarantees that you'll have to pay taxes on the money you take out? Would you choose the taxable bucket and have to pay taxes on your gains and on dividends when they're paid (even if you don't take the cash out of your account)? Or would you choose the tax-free bucket—the only one that legally allows you to keep all the money you take out, without sharing any with the IRS?

Now you understand why it's generally best to have your money coming out of the lowest-taxed vehicle possible so that more of your retirement income is spendable.

If you've read many books or websites that talk about financial planning, you've probably heard about the bucket strategy of retirement planning. The idea generally boils down to having assets spread out over three "buckets," one in cash or highly liquid investments (think money market accounts) so that you can pay for short-term needs and expenses, one with longer-term investments that are still relatively low-risk so you can use them for needs within the next five to ten years, and one with higher-potential, more-volatile, tax-deferred positions for far-out long-term cash needs.

This can be a valid asset allocation strategy, but without careful planning, the second and third buckets could be highly exposed to taxation once the assets are distributed. Ultimately, it doesn't matter how many buckets you split your assets up into if each of the buckets has a giant, IRS-shaped hole in the bottom.

THE BENEFITS OF TAX AND ACTUARIAL ARBITRAGE

Like tax arbitrage, *actuarial arbitrage* is really about where to put your money to get the most benefit. Arbitrage is such a fancy word but it's really quite simple: we all want to get the most benefit from what is ours and to take profitable advantages of the different options available to us.

We naturally want the option that provides the most financial benefit. Let's make up an example to illustrate this concept. Let's assume that you have the option of putting your money into one of two banks. You're planning on putting a large sum of money into the bank but over the next ten years you plan on taking out 90 percent of the account value. After ten years, only one tenth of the money you originally deposited remains, plus whatever interest you've earned along the way. The first bank, the Bank of Normal, offers you the following: 2 percent on your deposited amount and permission to take out one tenth of your money each year without any early withdrawal penalties. This 2 percent is not a bad offer, considering the low interest rates we currently have.

Thankfully, you check in with the other bank, the Friendly Bank. They are so friendly it's hard to believe. What they offer astounds you: you can earn interest when the economy is good and you can *never* lose any money if the economy turns sour. You'll pay no fees on your deposits, so the only time your account goes down in value is when you take money out of the account. You can access your money same as the Normal Bank *but* after the tenth year, because you've been so kind to trust them with your hard-earned money, they will actually pay you a pension for your entire life! Wow, that's pretty friendly, isn't it? Even better, if you are married you can make it a joint life pension so not only will this pension benefit you, but it can also benefit your spouse. And, if the economy is good, you get "pension credits" and your monthly payout actually goes up over time and once they increase your pension payout, they can never reduce it.

It's kind of a no-brainer that the Friendly Bank is just a better deal. Now, there's no Friendly Bank, but what I've described for you is a product that is used in a way that differs from how most advisors use it, resulting in a unique outcome that favors our clientele. These products come and go, but when we find a product that can be actuarially configured to provide an advantage to our clientele, we are swift about taking meaningful positions in them so the actuarial profits can accrue and work toward our client's long-term planning goals and objectives while minimizing, eliminating, or shifting as much risk as possible onto the issuer of the account and away from our client.

That's actuarial arbitrage! When you understand how to mix actuarial arbitrage with tax-distribution arbitrage, you end up with a very SMART retirement plan—one that affords you the advantage of Strategic Movement Around Retirement Taxation® as well as the earning potential created by actuarial float.

CHAPTER 4

GET SMART: ENJOY THE STRATEGIC MOVEMENT AROUND RETIREMENT TAXATION®

W hen I first got in this business twenty-five years ago, I was taught—and believed—that the worst place you could possibly be invested was in a taxable account. Why pay taxes when there were better options? After all, with a traditional IRA and 401(k) account we can defer the tax into the future and we'll probably pay less. I also believed that the best place in the world we could be was in a tax-free account. But, of course, the yields sometimes aren't high enough in tax-free accounts, so I believed that ideally a well-rounded retirement strategy should have some taxable, some tax-deferred, and some tax-free holdings. Either way, I was dedicated in my belief that the *worst* place of those three options was always a taxable account and paying tax now.

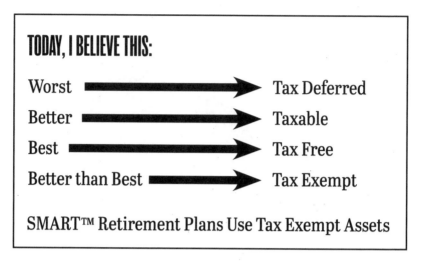

Fig. 23

Well, today I believe this: the worst place in the world you can be is tax deferred. I'll give you a minute to catch your breath because I know that comes as a shock to many of you, considering that the most popular retirement savings vehicle in America is, by far, the company-sponsored 401(k) plan.

Consider this: if tax rates go up significantly, most of us won't be able to out-earn the negative tax effects without taking considerable risk. That means it's possible that the balance of your IRA, 401(k), and other retirement accounts *today* is the most these accounts may ever be worth on a tax-adjusted basis. You see, as taxes increase, your net value goes down because you're essentially exposing these dollars (a.k.a., your future retirement income) to paying higher tax rates. That's why it's very likely that it's better to pay the tax now, when we know what we have to pay—especially since we're at historically low tax rates. Because I believe, as many of you do, that taxes are going to go up, which means if we pay taxes now we'll actually be paying at a discount compared to what we will likely pay in the future.

The next best choice, in my opinion, is to find a tax-free option. But it's still not always a perfect solution. Why? Well I've owned tax-free bonds before, and the bond broker told me they'd be income tax-free, and they were. But they weren't free from the alternative minimum tax, which turned my tax-free bonds into taxable bonds.

So what is the best option? Tax exempt. When you can find a way of creating tax-exempt income, it is the only way to truly create a tax-free income. The key to a SMART retirement plan is to find assets that truly are tax-free because of exemptions in the law. Now let's talk about how that's done.

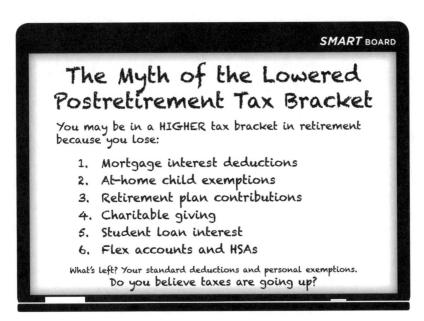

Fig. 24

This is the big fallacy that everyone is told: You'll be in a lower tax bracket in retirement. Well, guess what? That's not what we're seeing now, and here's why. When you're young or middle-aged and working, you have a lot of different deductions. You may be able to deduct interest on your house payments, exemptions for student loan interest, exemptions for dependent children who live with you, deductions and credits for retirement plan contributions, health coverage, and so on. And while retirees may have given charities monetary donations while they were working, now they give time. And guess what? Time is not a deductible expense. So what's left for seniors to deduct? Well, just the standard deduction. This is why most of the clients who were told they'd be in a lower tax bracket in retirement have found that they are *not* in a lower tax bracket, after all.

The SMART retirement planning strategy revolves around the strategic movement around retirement taxes. That means you have to dig deeper than simply believing the old adage that retired people pay less in taxes. Remember, your allowable deductions, exemptions, and credits are going to go down significantly when you're retired because chances are you will lose:

- **Dependents**: It's doubtful that you'll still have underage children to support while you're in retirement. You'll also lose all the associated tax breaks, such as those for childcare.

- **Mortgage interest**: It's never a good idea to head into retirement with debt, which likely means your home will be paid off before you leave the workforce. Even worse, as you age and pay down your principal, your mortgage interest expenses will be dropping dramatically, thereby increasing your taxes and possibly making it even harder to contribute to your retirement accounts.

- **Student loan interest**: Your student loans are likely to be paid off by the time you reach retirement, so no longer will you have that interest deduction to write off.

- **Retirement plan contributions**: Some accounts, such as the traditional IRA, have age limits for contributors. But even if you have accounts with no age limits, you still probably won't be contributing to retirement accounts when you no longer have an income.

- **Charitable giving**: Most retirees switch from donating money to donating time once they leave the workforce. Time is an amazing gift, but it's not tax deductible.

- **Flex accounts and HSAs**: As a retiree on Medicare, you won't have use for HSAs anymore and you'll have no employer offering a flex account, so you'll lose that excluded contribution. Worse, you may even begin taking qualified distributions from your HSA, which can increase your provisional income and may be subject to penalties.

At the time this book was updated, Donald Trump had just finished his first year in office. Upon his inauguration, many of us were expecting lower tax rates—and President Trump delivered on that campaign promise. Knowing that the new tax bill lowers tax rates for many, it may seem odd that I'm so focused on higher tax rates when talking about the SMART plan. But when I refer to higher tax rates, I'm talking about the imminent possibility of them rising over the whole of your retirement. If you are fifty years old, for example, and you have fifteen years before retirement and then another thirty or so years to enjoy retirement, that's a total of forty-five years that taxes will be adjusted through. Do you think you can count on every incoming administration to keep taxes low for the next forty-five years? I sure don't. And if that's the case, then it's even more important and advantageous to create your SMART plan now, so that if there are any tax consequences from conversions, you can pay them when tax rates are low and—for once—gain full ownership of your money. With proper redeployment, you can ensure you never pay taxes on those same funds again.

And let's just say that history doesn't repeat itself and we do, by some miracle, end up enjoying low tax rates for the next half-century. Taxes are taxes—no matter how low they are. They still take money out of your pocket and put it in someone else's, thus they are worth attempting to minimize. The SMART plan helps you move around any tax rates, even in this low-tax-rate fairytale scenario, and ultimately, keep more of *your* money.

THE FIRST STEP TO DESIGNING A SMART RETIREMENT PLAN

Match your deductions and exemptions to your retirement plan distributions

Standard deductions*	$12,000
Spousal deduction	$12,000
	$24,000

*For 2018, under 65

Fig. 25

The first step to designing a truly SMARTer retirement plan is to be aware of these deductions. The standard deduction as of 2018 for those under 65 is $24,000 for married couples and $12,000 for single filers. For those who are 65 or older, the standard deduction increases bringing it to $26,600 for married couples and $13,600 for single filers.

This is important to know because, if you are married and take out $24,000/$26,600 or less each year from your retirement plan (IRAs or 401(k)s), you'll pay no tax. It's just that simple. Sometimes when I teach these strategies about building your wealth by being more tax savvy, advisors want to take this to the extreme. But a SMART plan is all about balance. If you don't have a monthly defined pension benefit, and you just have an IRA and/or 401(k), you might be best off just to take that $24,000/$26,600 or less out a year and ultimately use that to offset your standard deduction , resulting in a tax-free, maximized distribution from your retirement plan. If you need more income than Social Security and $24,000/$26,600 from your IRA and/or 401(k), don't worry—we have more SMART techniques to deploy which we'll talk about in the next chapter.

So why isn't anybody out here really educating the public about matching deductions to retirement-plan sourced income? I don't know, but they should be—because it's pretty simple and is a vital first step.

Let's take a closer look at standard deductions.

• **Standard deductions**: This is the amount that all taxpayers who don't itemize are permitted to deduct from their gross income so that they have some amount of income that is protected from taxes. Since seniors lose out on many deductions (like the mortgage interest and charitable contributions), they will generally take the standard deduction because it's larger than the expenses they can legally include in an itemization. The standard deduction varies depending on your filing and marital status and it can be slightly larger for widows and widowers or those with certain visual impairments.

PROBLEM WITH 401K + IRAS: PROVISIONAL INCOME!

Provisional income example – Bill & Sally

50% of Soc. Sec benefit **$30,000** x ½	=	**$15,000**
Annual distribution from IRA	=	**$55,000**
Provisional income for SS tax purposes:		**$70,000**
At $70,000 prov. income, 85% of Soc. Sec. taxed		
85% x 30,000 = $25,500 @ 12% tax	=	**$3,060 Tax on SS!**
Total taxable income	=	**$56,500**
[$55,000 IRA + $25,500 SS – deductions ($24,000)]		
Tax on $56,500 taxable income	=	**$3,339**
Total **tax** due on actual income of **$85,000**	=	**$6,399**

Fig. 26

One big problem with 401(k)s and IRAs is provisional income. Provisional income is the calculation that's used to determine how much of your Social Security income is taxable. To really understand this concept, let's talk about Bill and Sally.

Bill and Sally take home $30,000[18] a year in Social Security benefits and $4,583 collectively per month in distributions from their IRAs. This gives them a total income of $85,000. Provisional income is determined by taking 50 percent of a retiree's Social Security benefit and adding it to their other sources of taxable income. The sum is then compared to IRS published tables (shown in Figures 27 and 28) and the taxable amount is determined. For Bill and Sally, that means that $15,000 of their Social Security income is added into this calculation along with the full $55,000 taken from their IRAs.

---

18   "Income from Social Security," Pension Rights Center, http://www.pensionrights.org/publications/statistic/income-social-security.

When you consider these two together for this calculation, their provisional income for determining Social Security taxation for Bill and Sally is $70,000. With $70,000 of provisional income, 85 percent of their Social Security will be taxed. Thus, you take 85 percent of their total $30,000 in Social Security income, and that equals $25,500 that they have to claim as taxable income on a benefit that was originally meant to be tax-free.

Let's assume that they're in a 12 percent tax bracket, which means they'll owe $3,060 in tax just on their Social Security income, which—again—was always intended to be a tax-free benefit. But that's only part of the story. Since they're also taking distributions from their IRA, their actual total taxable income is $56,500. At a 10 percent tax rate, that means they owe another $3,339 in taxes on that IRA income, bringing their annual tax bill up to around $6,339. That's a lot—especially if their spending burden is amplified due to increases in their supplemental health insurance premiums.

You might have found those last few sentences pretty confusing. I understand why; seriously, are Bill and Sally in a 10 percent tax bracket or a 12 percent tax bracket? Well … both actually.

You see, our income tax system is progressive and multi-dimensional so some of the earnings are in the 10 percent bracket and some cross over into the 12 percent federal bracket. With a progressive tax system, the tax calculations aren't based simply on the flat rates of each tax bracket. Without social security included, (a benefit that was intended to be tax-free when created) the average tax rate is 10.8 percent but with Social Security included, the actual tax rate becomes 11.3 percent.

Now, before we try to solve Bill and Sally's problem, I'd like to stop here for a moment and take a look at this. Is the answer here getting a higher rate of return or is it about being smarter about what's taxable and what's not taxable? Is it a smarter approach to figure out how to reposition our sources of income using tax arbitrage to create a better result? I'm going to show you that this is exactly the case in Bill and Sally's situation, but first let's take a look at a few charts that you need to know.

Married Couples	% Of Soc. Sec Taxed
Under $32,000	0%
$32,000 - $44,000	50%
Over $44,000	85%

Fig. 27

If you're a married couple, you want to strive, when possible, to keep your provisional income under $32,000 because that will ensure that none of your Social Security income is taxable. **Remember: This is not your full potential retirement income. You can still receive $1 million in tax-exempt income and have a $0 provisional income.**

If your provisional income is between $32,000 and $44,000, 50 percent of that Social Security income is taxed. If it's over $44,000, then 85 percent of your Social Security income is taxable. These are numbers that you need to know if you want to target your lowest potential tax rate. But remember—targeting the lowest potential rate doesn't mean that's all you earn. It's just about controlling what's taxable and reportable and what's not. A person receiving $80,000 per year from their Roth 401(k) and/or from cash-value life insurance would register at $0 for the Social Security provisional income tax thresholds. In this way, the SMART plan focuses on limiting your postretirement taxes—not your postretirement income.

dSMART RETIREMENT

Single & Widowers	% Of Soc. Sec Taxed
Under $25,000	0%
$25,000 - $34,000	50%
Over $34,000	85%

Fig. 28

If you're single or widowed, these numbers are lower. If your income is under $25,000, then your Social Security isn't taxed. If your provisional income is $25,000 to $34,000, then 50 percent of your Social Security is taxed. If your provisional income is more than $34,000, then 85 percent of your Social Security income will be taxable.

FIXING BILL AND SALLY

Move some money away from IRA to tax-exempt assets

50% of Soc. Sec benefit $30,000 x ½	=	$15,000
Annual distribution from IRA	=	$20,000
Tax-exempt income	=	$35,000
Provisional income for SS tax purposes:		**$35,000**
Provisional income	=	$35,000
$1,500 SS taxable + $20,000 IRA income	=	$21,500
– $24,000 Standard deduction		
Total tax due on $70,000 income	=	$0

Fig. 29

Let's go back to Bill and Sally and fix their problem. First, we want to move some money out of the IRA into Roth and tax-exempt

64

assets. That way, they can take just $20,000 in taxable income from the IRA and $35,000 in tax exempt income to get that full $55,000, but for the provisional income calculation, the only thing we would include is 50 percent of their Social Security ($15,000) and the taxable IRA distribution of $20,000, giving us a total provisional income of $35,000, which is over the $32,000 limit for married couples, making $1,500 of their Social Security income taxable. However, because they get a standard deduction of $24,000, the amount of total tax due would be zero.

Because tax-exempt income is just that, it's *exempt from taxation*, we have zero tax on the $30,000 of Social Security income and we've got zero tax on the $35,000 of tax-exempt income, which means the only reportable taxable income becomes $1,500 from Social Security and the amount that is being distributed from their IRA, which is $20,000. And for a married couple with $21,500 of income, the standard deduction will bring their total taxable income to $0.

So you can see where fixing Bill and Sally over time will provide a much better net spendable income for them in retirement, instead of the traditional planning methods. And while there will be taxes along the way to get there, they will be paid just one time. Better yet, the money that we save them in taxes will continue to compound and will ultimately be inherited by their family—truly tax-free.

FROM THE SMART WHYS TO
THE SMART HOWS

So how do we do this? We want to be smart about funding a SMART plan. The Roth IRA is wonderful, but there are some limitations to who can fund a Roth. These are some of those numbers for 2018: for married couples, the phase-out starts at $189,000 and ineligibility at $199,000. For singles, the phase-out begins at $120,000 and ineligibility is at $135,000. For those of you who are working toward retirement with income that falls below these limits, the Roth is a strong option. But it's not without its potential pitfalls, as Jim Lange, Esq. shares in his book, *The Roth Revolution: Pay Tax Once and Never Again*. With a Roth, you still bear investment risk, potential regulation changes and the risk of lower future tax rates.

Here's what happens if you're married with income over $199,000 or single with income over $135,000. Then you may want to consider a nondeductible IRA. Maybe. There are two different ways you can go about this. You can fund a nondeductible IRA and then convert it to a Roth, which may make sense if the money you contribute comes from your 401(k), 403(b), or 457. Your best option is to work with your employer and ask them to add a Roth 401(k) option to your company plan.

If, however, your retirement savings are primarily in a traditional IRA right now, you must approach this with extreme caution. The reason you don't want to try and convert traditional IRA funds to Roth IRA funds is that doing so can create excessive taxation on those dollars if other tax-deferred accounts, such as a 401(k), are in place but not being converted at the same time in the same proportions, which really defeats the purpose of the SMART plan. That's why you must avoid a do-it-yourself Roth conversion and instead make sure you're working with an advisor who understands your goals and knows the ins-and-outs of a SMART retirement plan. Roth conversions can be tricky and additional guidance from experts such as tax attorney Rick Law and his law partner Zach Hesselbaum, LLM are advisable. Further, detailed tax analysis is highly recommended by experts such as Stephen Biggie, CPA, a partner at the nationally recognized tax advisory and CPA firm Keebler & Associates.

The next question is how much to fund or to convert. The Internet is a helpful resource in many respects, but it's also limiting if you don't know what you're looking for or how to locate it. One way we see this over and over is in the prevalence of retirement calculators dotting the web landscape. These calculators claim to help users determine how much money they will need during retirement based on their anticipated expenses and, thus, how much they need to save at their anticipated rate of return.

Sadly, these calculators and really the whole approach of anticipating full future retirement income needs and focusing on how much to save, is lacking for several reasons. First, the Social Security numbers used by calculators are based on pure assumption and don't consider many of the problems facing Social Security as well as the very real possibility of future benefit rollbacks to compensate for the dropping ratio of workers to recipients.

Second, these calculators may assume that your returns will fluctuate, and they will unless you're completely invested in fixed products, but they have no way of anticipating how wildly they will fluctuate or in what years you might see no return or a negative return. This can be an extreme problem, which you saw in chapter 2.

A third problem with this process and these calculators is that they don't know how your tax situation will change as you age. They may not account for the losses in deductions you'll experience once you pay off debt and retire, and they have no idea what tax rates are going to do over the years.

Don't get me wrong, having retirement savings goals based on a loose idea of what you think you'll need is fine—it's just not the most important plan you need to make.

Instead, I suggest that we always seek to simply match our IRA and 401(k) distribution amounts to the standard deduction, assuming they aren't offsetting income coming to you from a defined benefit plan. Anything that's over that amount, we want to distribute from a Roth or tax-exempt source. But be careful about conversions so that you can avoid triggering excessive provisional income, making a large percentage of your Social Security benefits taxable. And remember, always get help before you do any conversions to avoid being taxed twice on existing IRA balances.

WHERE SHOULD YOU INVEST YOUR MONEY?

This question infers that finding the right investment for your money—so that you can accumulate more—is the key to ensuring your retirement security. Too many people think that the accumulation phase of retirement, which would be a lot like the phase of mountain climbing where you're hoisting yourself up the side of a cliff in an attempt to reach the summit, is the most important phase. But as I said earlier, planning for the descent is more important than the climb. When was the last time you heard about a mountain climber who wanted to climb a mountain and then never come back down again? Probably never. Planning only for your retirement accumulation is like planning for a mountain climbing trip by only preparing to go up the mountain, not to get down again. If you want to succeed, then you have to pack your bags right for both your retirement ascent and eventual descent.

When it comes to retirement planning, your actual retirement—those years when you're taking consistent distributions from your savings—that's the climb down the mountain. If you think about it, that's actually what all the prep was for. That is the stage of your retirement that determines your success, and that's the state that you want to make sure is successful. Every year, close to a thousand highly trained, experienced, and prepared mountain climbers try to scale

Everest, one of the world's tallest peaks—and only about half make it to the top.[19] Do you think the hundreds of climbers that don't make it are okay with also not making the climb down? Or do you think that at the point they realize they can't make it to the summit, their descent becomes their top priority—the part where they want to succeed, no matter how far they are from the summit? And of those who make it to the top, do you think that once they summit they stop caring about whether they'll make it down? Or do you think they take care to get down safely and in one piece?

Asking where you should put your money, and then leaving it at that, is like looking at the maps and topography, talking to other climbers, and working with Sherpas solely for the goal of reaching the top of Everest and then having no plan, equipment, or method for getting back down again.

I find that time, math, and money rarely move in the same direction. It is quite strange because the whole idea of compounding interest and capital appreciation are based on a rate of return compounded over time. In fact, the math for appreciation is based on four variables: present value, future value, rate of return, and time.

It follows, then, that time, money, and math should be aligned and earning more income for retirees and pre-retirees—right? Well, maybe. If you take risk with your money, values can go up—but they can also go down.

---

19   Mark Jenkins, "Everest Maxed Out," *National Geographic*, June 2013, ngm.nationalgeographic. com/2013/06/125-everest-maxed-out/jenkins-text.

Market historians and verified data offer long-term rates of return that are very attractive, yet when the economy gets rough, money can be (and has been) lost, which doesn't help folks and their families grow toward a stronger financial future.

When you factor in the growth of taxes over time, you have even more threats to your income and a greater chance to lose money, that is, unless you are SMART when planning and minimize your future tax liabilities. What else can you do to help stay on the right track regardless of how time wants to erode your money? Well, you can start by diversifying between many different types of assets. Avoid biases such as, "I only invest in mutual funds or just stocks and bonds." Also, don't build in a bias toward products you may not understand, such as: "I don't believe in life insurance." Allow yourself to be open to all possibilities— they all may have a lot of merit in a well-designed plan. Next, you should not try to time anything. Instead, build a great plan based on sound retirement planning principals and then stick with it. Allow time to work for you and do not allow your emotions to work against you and your money. Lastly, make sure you regularly review your plan. Keep track of where you are, what you have, and where you want your retirement planning to go. That is the ultimate key to utilizing time and achieving planning success.

THE MORAL OF THE STORY

I'm not saying or trying to imply that the question of what to invest in isn't worth asking or answering. It can be a meaningful part of your retirement planning, but focusing exclusively on that doesn't allow you to get a full picture of everything involved in designing a SMART retirement that creates a stable, tax-efficient income that *lasts*. Further, in a later chapter, I'll show you exactly what I personally own and why.

CHAPTER 5

SMART PEOPLE, SMART PLANS

For many people, the income available when sticking to the standard deductions simply isn't enough to live the lifestyle they want to live based on the wealth they've accumulated. Of course, after reading this book, they understand that trying to take more out of their tax-qualified and pre-tax retirement plans isn't really going to substantially increase their style of living so much as substantially increasing their annual tax bill. So what's a retiree to do? Why not take a look at a hundred-plus-year-old product that banks and billionaires can't get enough of?

High-cash-value, low-death-benefit life insurance—specifically, for me, it's 10-pay.

HIGHER INCOME WITHOUT TAXATION

WHY WHOLE LIFE INSURANCE?

→ Cash accumulated is accessible as tax-preferred income
→ No contribution limits
→ No income cap limitation
→ No provisional income
→ Safe harbor for legislative change ('82, '84, '88)
→ Benefits paid to family are tax-preferred
→ Waiver of contributions if disabled
→ Benefits for chronic care and terminal illness

Fig. 30

A 10-pay life insurance policy is called a limited-pay life insurance policy. It offers a lifetime of policy benefits after a set term of premiums deposits, in this case ten years. Depending on the type of coverage you choose, the policy can simply stay in-force after ten full premiums payments are made on a guaranteed and paid-up basis.

While the payments are stretched out over a certain term, this is not a term life policy—it's a high-cash-value, low-death-benefit policy offering a lifetime of benefits. That means that the death benefits are payable even if the insured passes away thirty years after they stopped making premium payments. It also means that the policy accrues significant cash values, which means you have access to cash that you can—no, that you *should*—use to make major purchases, replace bank financing, and ultimately distribute money from in your retirement via structured loans and, thus, without taxation. With the freedom this offers you, you can avoid using credit cards with their expensive interest rates and become your own bank—financing your own residence and vacation home loans without the tricky math used by traditional bank lenders.

You might be wondering why I'm talking about 10-pay insurance after bringing up the issue of income shortages for retirees. Here's the thing: with the right 10-pay policy, you're accruing significant cash that you can access after you've retired. That accumulated cash is always available to you and when you take it out, you can do so without any tax ramifications. It isn't counted as provisional income, so it doesn't offset your Social Security and trigger taxation and it itself isn't taxable.

There are also no contribution limits other than your ability to afford paying the premiums, which is easy if you dollar-cost average a less-tax-efficient asset into the 10-pay over that ten-year period. There is no income limitation, no required minimum distributions, and no conversions required. Ultimately, what I'm saying is that with a 10-pay life insurance policy, you never have to worry about the income you're taking out, because it's not going to trigger a tax if you keep the contract in-force. There is simply no 1099 or other tax reporting.

The most beneficial, high-cash-value policies have changed and evolved over time. The tax benefits are firmly rooted in the tax code and changes have always been brought forward, honoring prior law arrangements. Tax law changes around this class of product have always been grandfathered, because they happened in 1982, 1984, and 1988, when a lot of what we're going to show you today was even *more* readily available, with bigger amounts of early funding allowed and faster benefits. But the heart of the tax advantages of a high-cash-value life insurance policy are still very viable today through 10-pay policies:

- Income from high-cash-value policies can be completely tax-free.

- Death benefits paid to your family who inherit it when you're gone are completely tax-free.

- There is no contribution limit other than the maximum premium to avoid creating a *modified endowment contract*, a situation where cash values grow too quickly and the policy structure forfeits the tax-exempt nature of cash value, if accessed.

- There are riders, such as a waiver of premium for disability, that can allow premiums to be waived in the event of a disability.

- There are benefits for chronic care and terminal illness so you can leverage your policy benefits for those uncomfortable and unwelcome life realities.

You know, these things happen. Disability and long-term care and chronic illness are realities. This is a product that has leveraged benefits for those eventualities. Those are just some of the reasons I heavily fund, use, and love 10-pay for myself as a way to build tax-exempt assets.

WHY HIGH CASH VALUE LIFE INSURANCE?

Summary and Comparison of U.S. Bank Tier 1 Capital, Fixed Assets, Life Insurance, and Pension Assets as of September 30, 2013 in $$/Billions

Bank	Tier 1 Capital	Bank Premises Fixed Assets	Life Insurance Annuity Values	Defined Benefit Pension
Wells Fargo	$116.5	$7.59	$18.2	$9.2
JPMorgan Chase	$137.5	$11.1	$10.4	$14.0
Bank of America	$146.2	$9.2	$20.3	$17.7**
PNC Bank	$28.5	$4.6	$7.4	$4.2
Bank of NY Mellon	$15.7	$1.3	$3.7	$4.6

Source: Company reports, IRS 5500s

*FDIC as of December 31, 2013, defined benefits as of 9/30/2013
**Bank of America froze its defined-benefit pension as of February 2012

Fig. 31

But let's take a closer look at this. Why is it that Wells Fargo has $18.2 billion of life insurance and annuity cash values in its tier 1 capital? Tier 1 capital is the safest capital in the bank. They have more life insurance and annuity values on the book than they have money in their defined benefit pension plan to pay out for their future retirement benefits. They've got more of these values on their books than they have invested in physical bank buildings.

As of 2010, JP Morgan had $10 billion. Bank of America who owns Merrill Lynch had $20.3 billion. PNC Bank had $7.4 billion. And Mellon had $3.7 billion. These are huge amounts of money that they have in high-cash-value insurance-based products.[20]

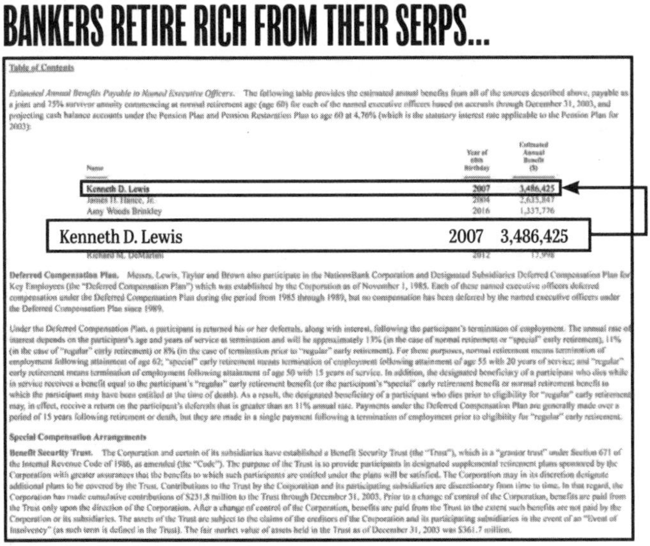

BANKERS RETIRE RICH FROM THEIR SERPS...

Fig. 32

Let's take a look at an individual example. Bank of America's CEO Ken Lewis is guaranteed to get $3.486 million a year as an annual retirement benefit beginning at age sixty. How do you think

20   Berry James Dyke, *Guaranteed Income: A Risk-Free Guide to Retirement* (Castle Asset Management, 2015).

Bank of America plans on fulfilling the promise of those benefits? Well, they're going to use what Bank of America refers to in their annual statement as a SERP. That stands for *Supplemental Executive Retirement Plan.* The SERP is *not* the company 401(k) or a defined benefit pension plan. It's a special plan for their most senior executives.

Fig. 33

On that corporate annual report, they show $53.4 million in Ken's SERP. What is that really? It's a high-cash-value life insurance policy. That's what they are using to ensure that they're able to make good on Ken Lewis's $3.4 million-a-year special pension. Let's think about that for a second.

Bank of America owns Merrill Lynch

Kenneth D. Lewis is the *Big Boss*

He is guaranteed $3,486,425 from BOA @ age 60

They have $53,485,337 in cash
value to meet that obligation

****6.5% Withdrawal Rate****

Bull photo courtesy Flickr user htmvalerio, used under
Creative Commons Attribution-NoDerivs 2.0 Generic (CC BY-ND 2.0)

Fig. 34

The big boss of Merrill Lynch, who would love to manage your retirement for you, was guaranteed $3.4 million a year from a $53.485 million cash-value life insurance policy back in 2010. That's a pretty amazing withdrawal rate, right about 6.5 percent.[21] That's about double what Morningstar told us we could safely withdraw each year. That's a big distribution number, and remember too, that the policy's death benefit proceeds are likely going to come back to the company completely tax-free. This is, of course, assuming that Bank of America is adhering to the very strict guidelines that are enforced on corporate-owned life insurance policies.

---

21   "Notice of 2004 Annual Meeting of Shareholders," Bank of America Corporation, https://www.sec.gov/Archives/edgar/data/70858/000119312504068314/ddef14a.htm.

Name	Company	Amount	Plan
Ken Lewis	Bank of America	$53 Mil	SERP
Randall Stephenson	AT&T	$41 Mil	SERP
James McNering	Boeing	$34 Mil	SERP
Muhtar Kent	Coca-Cola	$39 Mil	SERP
Brian Roberts	Comcast	$232 Mil	Split Dollar
Rex Tillerson	Exxon	$43 Mil	Add Pay Plan
Jeffrey Immelt	GE	$52 Mil	SERP
Samuel Palmisano	IBM	$28,894,991 $863,442	NQ Def Comp Qualified Plan
Marilyn Hewson	Lockheed Martin	$36 Mil	SERP

Source: Dyke, B. (n.d.). Guaranteed Income: A Risk-Free Guide to Retirement.

Fig. 35

Smart people are creating "SMART plans" for themselves—big company CEOs like Ken Lewis at Bank of America, with his $53 million in his supplemental executive retirement plan (SERP); Stephenson at AT&T with $41 million; Boeing's CEO McNerney with $34 million; Kent at Coca-Cola with $39 million; Roberts at Comcast with $232 million in what's called a split-dollar arrangement, yet another type of insurance-based plan; Exxon's Tillerson (our new secretary of state) with $43 million; GE's CEO with $52 million; and Palmisano over at IBM with $28.8 million in his non-qualified deferred compensation plan, which is also likely insurance based. Palmisano is the only one from Barry Dyke's research who had a 401(k) plan. The rest of them didn't.[22]

---

22   Barry James Dyke, *Guaranteed Income: A Risk-Free Guide to Retirement* (Castle Asset Management, 2015).

LOCKHEED MARTIN TO PAY $62 MILLION TO SETTLE 401K LAWSUIT

Source: http://fortune.com/2015/02/20/lockheed-martin-to-pay-62-million-to-settle-401k-lawsuit/

Fig. 36

Marilyn Hewson, the CEO down at Lockheed Martin, has $36 million in her supplemental executive retirement plan at a time when 108,000 of her employees are naming her and their pension board for the mismanagement of their 401(k).

It is interesting that, today, advisors are telling people more and more to put the oxygen mask on themselves, like when you're on a plane. Advisors are telling their clients to make sure they get all the income they need, don't worry about beneficiaries, don't worry about kids and grandkids. I have a real objection to that because I know these kids aren't going to get pension plans. They have 401(k)s. There are no guarantees in a 401(k). These kids—your loved ones, heirs, and beneficiaries—are not going to get Social Security, because Social Security is on the verge of bankruptcy sometime in 2030s. In the 2030s, it's either going away or is going to be replaced by something far less benefits rich. Does it mean no other system won't come along? I don't know. But it certainly won't be like the system that didn't work in the first place. So it's going to be a lesser system. Kids today have no guarantee from their employer, they have no guarantee from the government, and advisors have the audacity to make this all about you. I don't believe that is correct. Especially since I know for a fact that you can nearly double the distribution rates while keeping your principal intact and building your wealth, because the wealth that you perpetuate onto the next generation can be tax-free if you're willing to work a little bit harder and a little bit smarter—and you don't need to use the "only take care of yourself" approach suggested by income planners.

Kids today with student loans are strapped. They can't get ahead, and they're not going to have the same benefits that people have today. You also have people like these big CEOs, who really are taking care of themselves and not focused on the folks who work hard for them and have to manage their own 401(k) plan assets.

MYSTERY BILLIONAIRE BUYS RECORD-BREAKING $201 MILLION LIFE INSURANCE POLICY

Source: http://www.forbes.com/sites/natalierobehmed/2014/03/14/mystery-billionaire-buys-record-breaking-201-million-life-insurance-policy/#5fb34e6f78b6

Fig. 37

Still think maybe life insurance isn't a good choice? Then why did this mystery billionaire buy a record-breaking $201 million policy? Do you think this mystery billionaire needs to die with more money? Or is there another reason this policy might be beneficial to them?

JIM HARBAUGH, U-M AGREED TO ADDITIONAL $2 MILLION ANNUAL COMPENSATION IN JUNE

Source: http://www.freep.com/story/sports/college/university-michigan/wolverines/2016/08/17/michigan-jim-harbaugh-contract/88910306/

Fig. 38

Do you love football? Then you probably know who University of Michigan head coach Jim Harbaugh is. Jim's a smart guy, right? So how does he get a significant portion of his compensation? In the form of an annual life insurance premium, a $2 million annual payment to the insurance company for a period of seven years. It's estimated that, based on that $2 million annual premium, after they pay the expense of his plan back to the university at his death, there could be at least $20 million left, tax-free, for his wife, his kids, and his trust. This split dollar plan is going to support him in retirement (tax-free), it's going to pay back the school (tax-free), and it's going to leave his wife, his kids, and his trust with a large amount of completely tax-free wealth.[23]

Trusts aren't just for football coaches like Jim Harbaugh. They can benefit people like you and me, as well. There are four basic things that are essential in figuring out if a trust is right for you, or if the trust you already have is doing its job.

There are many types of trusts, but the most basic is a revocable trust, sometimes referred to as a living trust. A revocable trust is advisable when you have after-tax accounts (not your IRAs, 401(k)s, 403(b)s, or other pre-tax retirement plans), and you do not want them to go through probate. In most states, a revocable trust directs your estate privately, so there is neither a public announcement nor a judge involved in making sure your estate is settled without debt. A revocable trust can also distribute money over

23   Mark Snyder and Steve Berkowitz, "Jim Harbaugh, U-M agreed to $2-million additional compensation in June," *Detroit Free* Press, August 17, 2016, http://www.freep.com/story/sports/college/university-michigan/wolverines/2016/08/17/michigan-jim-harbaugh-contract/88910306/.

time, if your goal is to spread distribution to your family for many years after you pass away. Many times, we see trusts distributed this way when the grandchildren are young. As you can see, the benefits of using a revocable trust can be great. Revocable trust owners must be aware that if they become disabled, their successor trustee must follow their instructions. In essence, the trust can be revoked or changed by you, but your child who takes over in the event you are disabled does not have that same flexibility.

The biggest possible misstep with a revocable trust comes when you, as the grantor of the trust, become disabled and your adult child takes over when there is language specific to healthcare and your direction to pay for that care from your trust. In this situation, any protection of your assets from long-term care that your child could have used to protect your hard-earned dollars from a medical spend-down is lost.

Irrevocable trusts can have many strings attached. You need to know what those are before you enter into an agreement that cannot be changed without court involvement. Irrevocable trusts are great for holding life insurance outside of your taxable estate, if you have no intention of getting to your cash value in the future. Some irrevocable trust planning makes sense when certain types of real estate are involved. Experienced elder law attorneys know how to create hybrid trusts that offer some of the desirable benefits of an irrevocable trust, while offering more flexibility and fewer problematic strings attached.

You cannot wrap a trust around your IRA. Your IRA is a pre-tax asset, and it is directed at your death by beneficiary designations. It is critical that you keep a copy of your beneficiary designation form with your legal documents. In the event that you die and the custodian cannot find your IRA beneficiary designation, your IRA is paid to your estate and ends up becoming a probate asset that goes through the full process of probate. This cost and delay of probate can easily be avoided by maintaining a copy of your IRA beneficiary designation form.

In many situations, trusts make sense, but if the trusts are not funded, the benefits are lost. All too often a person seeks out the least-expensive trust option, desiring value for their money but end up getting absolutely nothing for their money. Once you have a trust, you must link it to the accounts you want governed by the terms and conditions of your trust (could be revocable or irrevocable). For instance, if you have a CD at Happy People's Bank for $100,000, and you want it to be distributed to your family through your revocable trust but the statement comes and it is your name on the account registration, then none of the benefits of the trust are realized. The CD will go through probate and the instructions you left behind after your death will be ignored. Funding a trust is not hard, but you need to take the time to make sure that all the institutions that hold your money have a copy of the trust that reflects the proper ownership of your assets to the trust and not to you, in your name individually, or jointly, if married.

Finally, it's essential that you get help from a qualified attorney who can confirm that the assets you own are, in fact, properly wired to your trust. Take some time to discuss your trust planning options, and when you decide they are right for you, make every effort to ensure they are properly attached to your assets so they ultimately go to those you love.

UNDERSTANDING THE CAPITAL EQUIVALENT OF DIFFERENT ASSETS

For just a moment, I want you to consider a $1 million IRA. Based on the report we read from Morningstar, our IRA owner would benefit by receiving $28,000 in annual income, before taxes. Let's assume a tax rate of 20 percent total. This gives us $5,600 in taxes and a net retirement income of $22,400.

Now let's say that instead of having a $1 million IRA, we implemented some SMART thinking before retirement and took money out of the IRA, over time and after tax, and with only modest growth we ended up with $750,000 of cash value in a 10-pay whole life insurance policy.

Now, on the surface, this doesn't look very SMART—I mean, we have $250,000 less money! That can't possibly be SMART, can it? Well, actually, it depends on your goal. Because remember, we have to climb down the retirement mountain—and if your goal is to do so while maximizing your retirement income, lifestyle, enjoyment, and estate value for your family, then yes, it actually *is* SMARTer to have less *because you and everyone you love gets more!*

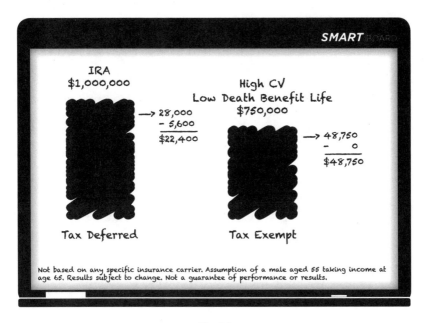

Fig. 39

As you can see from Figure 39, when we assume the distribution rate is equal to other, similar plans like those we discussed before, you can see that a properly funded 10-pay policy with a top-quality mutual insurance company, historically speaking, can sustain a distribution rate of 6.5 percent. This may be similar to the way Ken Lewis's SERP was structured at Bank of America. The policy also provides a significant death benefit through normal-aged mortality at an amount superior to the after-tax value of the IRA account.

So how can you compare an apple to an orange? After all, *tax deferred* is not *tax exempt*, and *tax exempt* certainly isn't *tax deferred*. So instead, let's consider a capital equivalent. How much money would we need to have in a tax-deferred account to net us the same after-tax income amount provided by the tax-exempt asset? Well, we know from the illustrations at the current dividend rate that the insurance policy is giving us $48,750 per year.

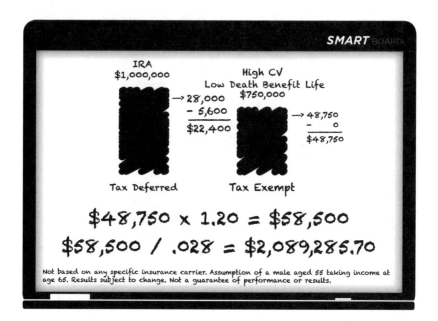

Fig. 40

That's right—if we consider the Morningstar safe withdrawal rate of 2.8 percent, we would need more than twice as much capital in a tax-deferred account to get distributions that are, after tax, equal to those from the tax-exempt product. Double the capital!

As you can see, if you're planning to live off of your money in retirement, the math dramatically favors tax-exempt distribution. And this is looking solely at a 20 percent tax rate. It's going to get even harder, and require even more capital, to get the same results if you only have a tax-deferred account and tax rates go higher—which is what I expect. And don't forget—with the tax-exempt, 10-pay life insurance option, you have the death benefit, which is higher than your cash value, going to those you love, tax free.

CHAPTER 6

MY PERSONAL SMART PLAN

Right now, I want you to take a look at my 10-pay policy—because yes, I have one as part of my own SMART plan. But first I want to say that no two people or families have the same situation. I share a portion of my plan with you to be transparent, not because I think everyone can benefit from the same exact solution. After all, a one-size-fits-all approach is never smart. Mostly, I share this with you because I want you to know this isn't a flavor of the month. This is what we do and we do it well because we believe in what we do and put our own money where our advice goes.

That said, each reader of this book is in a different situation than me—different age, different income, different asset base, different circumstances, and different goals. Some of you would fund less than me; others, a lot more. This example gives you some insight into how these plans work. I'd add this is a portion of my plan. I fully fund my Roth 401(k) every year; I have a small stock account for playing around with; I own physical gold (and silver) and oil and gas property. I also own rental real estate. The point I'm trying to make here is that this shouldn't be viewed as a single-solution plan. It would be better for you to think of properly funded high-cash-value life insurance as a financial warehouse where money waits to be deployed as new opportunities present themselves. Money I take from my life policies always finds its way back to the warehouse, so my dividends and paid-up additions can continue to grow my cash values and death benefits—both of which are growing tax-free.

I'd also add that this is the **only** asset I own that continues to get funded through a waiver of premium optional rider if I become disabled. Once again, this is a choice I made because it made sense for me. And to tell you the truth, it's comforting for me to know that if I become disabled, the money will continue to be contributed to my policy *by the carrier*. My Roth 401(k) contributions won't continue and be made by someone else. I won't buy any more stocks, gold, land, or rental real estate with funds provided by someone else. The only guarantee I have for continued funding if I am disabled is through my 10-pay policy. The policy also has a chronic illness and terminal illness rider to allow access to the death benefits during my life if something goes very wrong with my health. I hope I don't need any of those benefits, but they are there and it gives me some comfort in knowing that if things do go wrong for me, then the people I love and care for can go on without unjust financial burdens because I've taken care of myself *and* them.

LET'S LOOK AT MY 10-PAY POLICY
What's the *worst* thing that can happen?

Dur	End of Yr Age	Year	Annualized Current Policy Premium	Annualized Premium Outlay	Guaranteed Values		Net Death Benefit
					Cash Surrender Value		
1	47	2017	65,000.01	65,000.01	0		1,476,927
2	48	2018	65,000.01	65,000.01	38,489		1,476,927
3	49	2019	65,000.01	65,000.01	101,081		1,476,927
4	50	2020	65,000.01	65,000.01	166,140		1,476,927
5	51	2021	65,000.01	65,000.01	233,694		1,476,927
6	52	2022	65,000.01	65,000.01	303,878		1,476,927
7	53	2023	65,000.01	65,000.01	376,675		1,476,927
8	54	2024	65,000.01	65,000.01	452,265		1,476,927
9	55	2025	65,000.01	65,000.01	530,704		1,476,927
10	56	2026	65,000.01	65,000.01	612,083		1,476,927
11	57	2027	0.00	0.00	631,104		1,476,927
12	58	2028	0.00	0.00	650,601		1,476,927

Company has paid dividends continuously for ninety-two straight years and has been AM Best Rated A+ for fifty-one straight years.

Hypothetical insurance illustration. Does not represent a specific product or insurance carrier.

Fig. 41

Now let's look at my 10-pay policy and ask ourselves one vital question: What's the worst thing that can happen? This policy was issued by a company that's been rated A+ by A.M. Best for fifty-one continuous years. This mutual company has also paid dividends out to policyholders for ninety-two straight years in a row. They paid dividends to their policyholders through the Great Depression, through the energy crisis and bad market of 1973 and 1974, through the tech bubble, and even through 2008 when everything fell apart for the Great Recession. They paid dividends through all of those periods of economic turmoil. But just in case—*just in case*—they provide a "worst-case scenario" to show me what my policy will be worth if they suddenly stop paying dividends. And by the way, they have the right to do that. Of course, as I said, they haven't done that a single time in ninety-two consecutive years, but we're talking about worst-case scenarios here.

Remember earlier when we talked about basis? If we take a look at my policy, you can see that I paid $65,000 a year into the policy for ten years. That means I've paid a total of $650,000 over ten years. That's my basis. Our priority there is to make sure that basis is accounted for so it can be protected so that we are ensured a return of our capital and, hopefully, added gains through accumulated dividends. Now, granted, this worst-case guaranteed value isn't ideal, but at the end of twelve years this company has guaranteed me that they will have a definite cash value for me of $650,601. And if I die along the way, they're obligated to pay my beneficiaries $1,476,927. If I get disabled in year 4 (or in any year after the contract is issued), then the insurer is obligated to pay premiums for me over those remaining six years, so not only am I guaranteed the return of my capital but I also enjoy peace of mind knowing that I have other benefits and protections as well.

Again, this isn't ideal, nor is it my expected outcome, but at the end of twelve years the policy issuer has a statutory obligation to have guaranteed cash value for me of $650,601 and on top of that, they're obligated to pay my beneficiaries $1,476,927. So I have some real and valuable benefits that I can absolutely count on. This is literally the absolute worst thing that could happen to me. Now I'm guessing if it's this bad, it's likely the market's been a lot less kind to my neighbors and friends, right? But I know I can at least get my money back over twelve years based on the guarantee, my absolute worst-case scenario. Think about this for a moment; what kind of economic disaster would it take for this company to stop paying dividends for twelve straight years? How bad would things have to get—they didn't even stop paying dividends during the Great Depression! But let's say things do get that bad, so bad that our worst-case scenario here comes true. Now while I'm getting my paid-in premiums returned to me—what do you think is happening to my friends and neighbors who are invested in the stock and bond markets? They're lucky if they're getting back a small percentage of what they put in. But, no matter what, no matter how bad things get or how many market crashes we endure in the future, I know I can at least get my money back over twelve years based on that guarantee.

THE NEGATIVE SIDE OF LIFE INSURANCE

Why do people and advisors get so negative on life insurance? Well, first of all, there are a lot of different types of insurance contracts, and the best-fitting contract isn't always sold. When the wrong policy is sold in the interest of creating profit for an insurance agent and company, it makes the whole industry look bad—even if those policies may be a fit for other people.

One example is when universal insurance policies are sold without the buyer understanding that the cost of coverage—like the premium—is flexible. In my case, having a whole life policy, I don't have flexible premiums and the cost component is actuarially set at the time of purchase, yet there is still a "knock." And the "knock" is it has a bad rate of return. That's it. Your guaranteed asset, which guarantees *at minimum* a return of your basis over a period of time, has a bad rate of return. And whenever someone throws that bad rate of return argument at me, the first thing I do is ask them what's bad about having a guaranteed asset? What's bad about having something that will pay the ongoing obligation for you if you become disabled? What's bad about having a chronic and terminal illness rider? Especially since this so-called bad rate of return is literally only in year 1—one, single year! Let's look at the numbers.

LET'S LOOK AT MY 10-PAY POLICY
Accumulation: Bad Rate of Return!

Annualized Premium Outlay	Cumulative Premium Outlay	Total Dividend	Cumulative Dividends	Cash Surrender Value	Net Death Benefit
65,000.01	65,000	5,878	5,878	5,878	1,495,935
65,000.01	130,000	6,214	12,092	50,779	1,515,374
65,000.01	195,000	6,696	18,788	120,481	1,535,637
65,000.01	260,000	7,371	26,159	193,563	1,557,217
65,000.01	325,000	8,202	34,361	270,239	1,580,453
65,000.01	390,000	9,284	43,645	350,925	1,605,904
65,000.01	455,000	10,621	54,266	435,898	1,634,090
65,000.01	520,000	12,300	66,566	525,723	1,665,699
65,000.01	585,000	14,478	81,044	631,013	1,701,741
65,000.01	650,000	17,480	98,525	722,733	1,743,920

Hypothetical insurance illustration. Does not represent a specific product or insurance carrier.

Fig. 42

Remember how I told you rate of return was only half the story? Let's take a look at the other half. Here's what they mean by bad rate of return. On the accumulation basis, $650,000 has been paid in, which is the cumulative premium outlay, and at the end of year 10 the cash surrender value is $722,733 under the current dividend scale. Ignoring the fact that my death benefit has also grown during this time, if you just do the math on my cash value, it's not a great rate of return. It's possible that I could have accumulated even more using traditional retirement planning assets, such as mutual funds or stocks. But you know what else is possible in that scenario? That I could have lost a sizeable portion of my money—or even lost it all in those more traditional retirement planning assets.

What people really hate is that first year, when the cash surrender value is so low compared to the premium funded into the contract.

But what no one likes to talk about (or consider the possibility of) is the fact that I could die in that first year, and then the policy would have to pay out over $1.4 million to my beneficiaries. And if I become disabled in year 1, then they have to pay $65,000 a year for nine years into my policy on my behalf. So it's not that you've lost money or your money has disappeared in that first year, it's that it simply isn't accessible to you. It's being used to secure other benefits—including future, assured benefits. Like any good business, nothing happens in a short period of time. It takes time. With a product that's called *whole life*, it takes a period of time to accumulate, but it's incredibly beneficial for your entire life.

Let's talk about what really matters. I do agree that the rate of return is initially low, and I don't try to hide that. But we don't live on rate of return in retirement—we live off of the withdrawal rate. And the withdrawal rate on a properly structured 10-pay contract is nothing short of amazing to me. What you're going to see here is you can look at withdrawal rates of 6 to 7 percent on a 10-pay policy, as opposed to the safe withdrawal rate of 2.7 percent Morningstar told us we could take from a market-based retirement plan. Now things get a little bit different, don't they? Please understand, these rates are reasonable to assume today in our current interest rate environment. Could they be lower? Sure, but I'd argue there is an equal—if not greater—chance that they can be higher.

ACCUMULATION PHASE

	End of Yr		Annualized Current Policy	Annualized Premium	Cumulative Premium	Current Values			
Dur	Age	Year	Premium	Outlay	Outlay	Total Dividend	Cumulative Dividends	Cash Surrender Value	Net Death Benefit
1	47	2017	65,000.01	65,000.01	65,000	5,878	5,878	5,878	1,495,935
2	48	2018	65,000.01	65,000.01	130,000	6,214	12,092	50,779	1,515,374
3	49	2019	65,000.01	65,000.01	195,000	6,696	18,788	120,481	1,535,637
4	50	2020	65,000.01	65,000.01	260,000	7,371	26,159	193,563	1,557,217
5	51	2021	65,000.01	65,000.01	325,000	8,202	34,361	270,239	1,580,453
6	52	2022	65,000.01	65,000.01	390,000	9,284	43,645	350,925	1,605,904
7	53	2023	65,000.01	65,000.01	455,000	10,621	54,266	435,898	1,634,090
8	54	2024	65,000.01	65,000.01	520,000	12,300	66,566	525,723	1,665,699
10	**56**	**2026**	**65,000.01**	**65,000.01**	**650,000**	**17,480**	**98,525**	**722,733**	**1,743,920**
11	57	2027	0.00	0.00	650,000	15,918	114,443	761,217	1,781,166
12	58	2028	0.00	0.00	650,000	17,091	131,533	801,712	1,819,964
13	59	2029	0.00	0.00	650,000	18,339	149,873	844,475	1,860,365
14	60	2030	0.00	0.00	650,000	19,744	169,617	889,688	1,902,588
15	61	2031	0.00	0.00	650,000	21,192	190,809	937,326	1,946,598
16	62	2032	0.00	0.00	650,000	22,756	213,565	987,451	1,992,516
17	63	2033	0.00	0.00	650,000	24,419	237,983	1,040,044	2,040,422
18	64	2034	0.00	0.00	650,000	26,155	264,139	1,095,132	2,090,346
19	65	2035	0.00	0.00	650,000	27,938	292,077	1,152,837	2,142,262

Hypothetical insurance illustration. Does not represent a specific product or insurance carrier.

Fig. 43

DISTRIBUTION PHASE

	End of Yr		Annualized Premium	Cumulative Premium	Current Values			
Dur	Age	Year	Outlay	Outlay	Total Dividend	Cumulative Dividends	Cash Surrender Value	Net Death Benefit
20	66	2036	-80,000.00	570,000	29,820	321,896	1,129,588	2,112,559
21	67	2037	-80,000.00	490,000	31,768	353,664	1,105,426	2,081,072
22	68	2038	-80,000.00	410,000	33,808	387,472	1,080,398	2,047,664
23	69	2039	-80,000.00	330,000	35,943	423,415	1,054,458	2,012,193
24	70	2040	-80,000.00	250,000	38,154	461,569	1,027,633	1,974,466
25	71	2041	-80,000.00	170,000	40,563	502,132	999,753	1,934,487
27	**73**	**2043**	**-80,000.00**	**10,000**	**45,971**	**591,264**	**940,219**	**1,847,670**
28	74	2044	-80,000.00	-70,000	48,974	640,238	908,125	1,800,777
29	75	2045	-80,000.00	-150,000	52,236	692,474	874,661	1,751,560
30	76	2046	-80,000.00	-230,000	55,722	748,196	839,777	1,699,962
31	77	2047	-80,000.00	-310,000	59,464	807,660	803,499	1,645,945
32	78	2048	-80,000.00	-390,000	63,388	871,048	765,503	1,589,360
33	79	2049	-80,000.00	-470,000	67,462	938,510	725,369	1,530,007
34	80	2050	-80,000.00	-550,000	71,767	1,010,277	682,714	1,467,793
35	81	2051	-80,000.00	-630,000	76,155	1,086,432	637,192	1,402,416
36	82	2052	-80,000.00	-710,000	80,695	1,167,127	588,331	1,333,664
37	83	2053	-80,000.00	-790,000	85,351	1,252,478	536,058	1,261,259
38	84	2054	-80,000.00	-870,000	90,134	1,342,612	480,169	1,184,921
39	85	2055	-80,000.00	-950,000	95,093	1,437,705	420,239	1,104,422
40	86	2056	-80,000.00	-1,030,000	100,264	1,537,969	355,726	1,019,574

Hypothetical insurance illustration. Does not represent a specific product or insurance carrier.

Fig. 44

Take a look at how my policy performs. You are looking at $80,000 a year coming out, and my basis by the age of seventy-three being reduced to just $10,000. Now if I live long enough to see age eighty-six and I take $80,000 a year out of this policy, I will have taken a $1 million *more* from the insurance company than I put in. Even better, if you look to the far right on the death benefit basis, the insurance company is still obligated to pay my beneficiary over a $1 million. At age seventy-three, I'll still have $10,000 left in the policy. That means I will have given them $10,000 more than they had given back to me. And, again, remember on that $80,000 I took out each year, I paid no tax, but if I died at that time, my beneficiaries would walk away with $1.847 million, tax-free.

TAPPING INTO LIFE INSURANCE DIVIDENDS:
It takes time but it's *so* worth it!
At 65 → $80,000/Yr. 100% tax exempt

Exempt from: Federal tax
                State tax
                Local tax
                Medicare premium cancellation
                Provisional income for Social Security taxation

No 1099!

Fig. 45

Tapping into a properly structured whole life dividend takes time, but it is so worth it. At age sixty-six, I'm looking at $80,000 a year, 100 percent tax-exempt. Exempt from federal tax, state tax, local tax, Medicare premium cancellation equations, provisional income for Social Security taxation, and there is no 1099 at all.

When you begin to take income out of a 10-pay policy, the withdrawals can be structured as either surrenders to basis or loans. In the case of a whole life policy, like mine, often the loan rate is lower than the dividend payment, which means you're essentially taking the loan interest free—and may even continue to make gains because your credited dividend continues to buy paid-up additions, growing your cash value and death benefit beyond the cumulative effect of the loan. When this is the case, loans outperform surrenders to basis. The most important thing to understand is that both types of distributions are tax-free. Later, I'll show you the actual tax code regarding this and explain why this is the case. It's not a loophole— it's a perfectly logical and legal move.

DOLLAR MULTIPLE RETURNS: THE FAMILY GROWTH FACTOR

@ age 73 remaining basis of $10,000
Death benefit of $1,847,670
That is **$184.76 for every $1** of basis

@ age 86 remaining basis of NEGATIVE $1,030,000
Death benefit of $1,019,547
Infinite return, cannot calculate

• Took over a million **beyond** basis
• Left over a million for family

Is one "BAD YEAR" worth it for all of that?

Fig. 46

So what's the growth factor here? Let's think about it from a family perspective. We'll call it the *Family Growth Factor* and the multiple dollars of return per dollar invested. At age seventy-three,

I would only have $10,000 of my own money still in this contract, with a death benefit of $1.847 million for my beneficiaries. That means I'm picking up $184.76, tax-free, for every $1 that I paid in. That's a phenomenal rate of return.

At age eighty-six, it becomes incalculable because I have a negative basis. I've literally put my money in, I've funneled it out during my whole life, and I've taken $1,030,000 more out of that policy than I ever put in, and the insurance company *still* owes my beneficiaries more than a $1 million—tax-free.

Gandhi once said, "It is health that is real wealth and not pieces of gold and silver." I can't help but wonder, though, if Gandhi knew about high-cash-value life insurance, he might have more simply said, "Health is real wealth." Even if you don't have health, however, and likely can't get approved for a life policy, your spouse might. You can insure a spouse or other individual you have an insurable interest in and float their future death benefit for your retirement income in the same way Buffett invests in the float of other companies. Take a look at this excerpt from an article in *The Actuary*:

> *Perhaps more intriguing is the huge discount to equity plus float of Munich Re. Adding back the roughly €40 billion float in its general insurance and reinsurance operations to its equity (including equity in its large life and health businesses, which is conservatively calculated) gives a total of over €60 billion. This is about three times its market capitalisation of €22 billion. Taxation of investment returns and a deteriorating reinsurance market no doubt account for much of the gap. However, it is conceivable that the shares might be undervalued. Berkshire's significant shareholding in Munich*

Re, the high dividend yield and the company's continual repurchasing of its own shares might support that view.[24]

Now, dividends can change. That means these numbers can be different than illustrated, but let me tell you, these numbers are estimated *conservatively* based on where the insurance company is today and their belief about where the economy will be in the future. In better interest rate times, they could perform even better. So you can't even calculate how much we get beyond basis with a properly structured 10-pay. And what are you really giving up? Well, it's one bad year—one bad year to get all of these benefits.

HOW CARRIERS MAKE HIGH-CASH-VALUE LIFE INSURANCE

People often ask me, but aren't these based on bonds? How in the world can a 10-pay dividend be higher than the current bond yield? I want to help you understand why this is such a great asset for you to have in your portfolio and why so many high-net-worth folks today are utilizing high-cash-value whole life insurance. It's simple. When you buy into a 10-pay contract, your yield is based on the insurance company's general account yield. Within that general account, they have bonds that go back as far as thirty years. Bond rates may be low now, but even just ten years ago they were much higher. Thirty years ago, they were much better—a lot better than today. So you have to consider the fact that buying into a 10-pay policy means buying into a vast bond portfolio with a long history and bonds with much larger coupon rates than today's issues have. Essentially, you're getting a piece of a mature, diversified, and well-managed portfolio that's been around for thirty years. Not a thirty-millisecond bond

---

24   "Insurance: Float-Based Valuations," The Actuary, www.theactuary.com/archive/old-articles/part-4/insurance-3A-float-based-valuations/.

trade. You don't want to be buying a bond if there's a bomb going off somewhere, and you don't want to be in the market if something's happening that could cause a market crash. If interest rates go up, then bond prices go down. Very rarely have we ever seen a time when the stock market and the bond market are simultaneously at all-time highs. These are new-age economic risks that old strategies can't protect against. Ironically, it's my belief that an insurance product that is older than the US tax code itself offers us a viable solution for these new-world economic challenges.

But there are added benefits. You see, with a properly structured mutual insurance company policy, you can make actuarial profits. These are a part of the dividends that are paid *to* you. Let's say someone buys a dollar's worth of non-participating coverage. An actuary says, "We need eighty-two cents to make good on this promise." So the CEO has eighteen cents of every premium dollar collected to work with. The CEO figures out that to pay for the buildings, keep the lights on, and keep everything working the way that he wants, the insurance company needs twelve cents. That means he has six cents left over. Who gets paid that extra six cents? The mutual participating policyholders. The reason is mutual companies don't have stockholders, so your 10-pay policy gets credited with this excess as a dividend. Whose policies *don't* get credited? The people who bought non-participating policies like term, universal and variable life. They don't get anything. And as much as I hate to see people sabotage their own retirement success with non-participating products, I know that when they're sold through the mutual insurers that I prefer for 10-pay, they will help increase the actuarial profits and my clients will end up with that gain in their policies due to the higher resulting dividend. Plus, the conservative approach taken by actuaries usually means they've set the premium higher than needed, and with 10-pay, you recapture that tax-free in your dividend.

Not only do the participating policyholders get a dividend on a regular basis, because again remember—this particular company that I favor has been paying dividends for ninety-four consecutive years and other quality mutual insurers have paid dividends for over a hundred straight years—but these mutual insurance companies may earn even more during years when the stock market and economy are struggling. Because when things go bad, people flee to safety, and one of the safest places to put your money (the *safest* place, in my opinion) is with an A+ rated mutual insurance carrier. That means more premiums being paid in, and, likely, more dividends declared.

In fact, in really bad times we may be looking at dividends that are not only being supported at current levels but potentially rising, depending on what's going on at the company and with interest rates at that time. It's a wonderful place for you to put your safe money. It's a great place for you to buy thirty years of bond history instead of trying to buy into the flavor of the day that can turn on you in a minute.

CHAPTER 7

IS IT YOUR TIME TO GET SMART?
I HOPE SO. HERE'S WHY.

can offer you two simple reasons to add a SMART
component to your planning immediately:

1. You really should consider taking advantage of float.
    You can achieve results using a personal financial
    version of float—much like Warren Buffett does at
    the corporate level at Berkshire Hathaway.

2. You'd also be SMART to find a tax-free source of capital
    that can be transferred to you to supplement your
    postretirement income. Now take a look at page twenty-
    seven from the *United States General Accounting Office
    Report to the Chairman, Committee on Finance, US Senate,
    and the Chairman Committee on Ways and Means, House of*

Representatives on the Tax Treatment of Life Insurance and Annuity Accrued Interest.

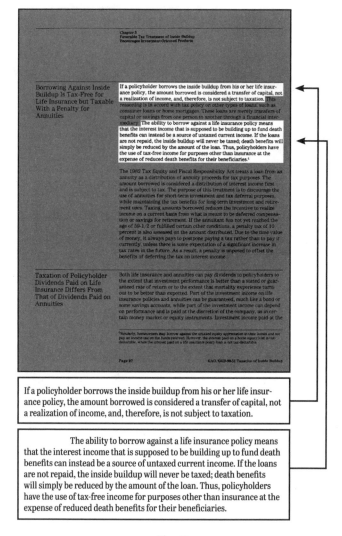

If a policyholder borrows the inside buildup from his or her life insurance policy, the amount borrowed is considered a transfer of capital, not a realization of income, and, therefore, is not subject to taxation.

The ability to borrow against a life insurance policy means that the interest income that is supposed to be building up to fund death benefits can instead be a source of untaxed current income. If the loans are not repaid, the inside buildup will never be taxed; death benefits will simply be reduced by the amount of the loan. Thus, policyholders have the use of tax-free income for purposes other than insurance at the expense of reduced death benefits for their beneficiaries.

Fig. 47

You'll accomplish both of these things by implementing a SMART plan. What I am about to share with you is a method to create tax-free income to live off of in retirement taken from the float from your death benefit. Yes, I am saying you can take tax-free distributions financed off of the value of your future dead self . . . creepy, I know, but let's look at what the GAO says right here in their tax policy about the tax treatment of life insurance to see exactly how this is done.

Many advisors get excited by this sentence right here:

> If a policyholder borrows the inside buildup from his or her life insurance policy, the amount borrowed is considered a transfer of capital, not a realization of income, and therefore, is not subject to tax.

But for me, it's this sentence in the GAO report that explains *how* you can profit from float, much like Warren Buffett does, that's exciting.[25] That sentence reads:

> The ability to borrow against a life insurance policy means that the interest income that is supposed to be building up to fund a death benefits can instead be a source of untaxed current income.

Now it gets even more specific here when it says:

> If the loans are not repaid, the inside buildup will never be taxed; death benefits will simply reduce the amount of the loan. Thus, policyholders have the use of tax-free income for purposes other than insurance at the expense of reduced death benefits for their beneficiaries.

That is exactly how you benefit from float and create tax-free income for yourself in retirement and still leave a significant tax-free inheritance to your family. **But take notice: this isn't a free lunch. There is an expense. Your eventual death benefit will be smaller**

---

25   US General Accounting Office, "Tax Treatment of Life Insurance and Annuity Accrued Interest," www.gao.gov/assets/150/148632.pdf.

based on your untaxed distributions. It's important to understand this isn't a loophole; it is a decision to forfeit a portion of one benefit in favor of another.

It is incredible that more people aren't aware that with a properly constructed 10-pay life policy you can, in fact, receive significant tax advantaged income, exempt from 1099s at *any time*—either before you retire or during your retirement—from the future value of your death benefit. This is you floating the value of your future dead self to live more financially well off today and potentially leave more generously to the people you love most when you die. SMART is simple, it just takes more effort on the part of the advisor who serves you, while looking out for your best interests.

My discovery of the SMART plan was much like your own was. It was all about the math—just as I've shown you in this book. For me, I place my trust in math over markets. The math here suggests you can live better in retirement and leave more wealth to those you love—and that is really what SMART is all about.

TIME TO GET SMART

After reading this, you may be wondering if this is your time to get SMART. The easy answer is that there is no *wrong* time to create a plan that focuses on the Strategic Movement Around Retirement Taxation®. Not only is it never too late to get started, but with the power of compounding at play, it's never too soon!

SMART isn't the traditional planning path popularized by big banks and Wall Street. It's a basis-focused approach to compounding your wealth by floating the insurance company's long-term liability payable to you at your death and instead tapping into it as a current untaxed income at the expense of a larger death benefit later. It's not a loophole—it's common sense. The tax authority has this right: give up some future death benefit to get some advantageous income. So why not go ahead and get started? Get SMART and get financially ahead—today.

To learn more about SMART, contact the advisor who gave you this book. If you purchased this book on your own, you can visit SmartRetiree.com to find resources and professionals who can help you get SMART!

ABOUT THE AUTHOR

Matt Zagula, founder of Zagula Management, likens his professional journey to the mountain climb that retirees make. Matt spent years accumulating knowledge from many different perspectives with the idea that when he finally hit that pinnacle of the mountain he would be well prepared to distribute quality advice that could be accounted for mathematically and not rely on hypothetical market illustrations. His goal was, and remains, to provide advice with confidence based on fact—not fiction.

Matt has followed a unique path, from being a very early adopter and pioneer in what is known today as income planning, to creating a distinctive practice model and level of notoriety in the industry that allowed his firm to be acquired in 2001, when Matt was just thirty-one, by a publicly traded company, National Financial Partners (NYSE Symbol: NFP), for stock and cash valued at over $1 million. In 2008, when the market tanked, Matt purchased his firm back from NFP and remains independent to this day.

Today, Matt is focused on helping pre-retirees and those in retirement get *more*—more income, more financial freedom, and more peace of mind knowing their plans are built on a solid foundation using the SMART Retirement Planning Process. Matt has spent decades continually adapting and evolving that model, and today he is considered to be a thought leader and planning innovator for tax, estate, and retirement income advanced designs. He is also the leading expert in tax and actuarial arbitrage.

Matt is dedicated to helping people and business owners profit from differences in the way their money is treated for tax purposes. Actuarially, he helps them realize profits by reversing the traditional use of certain insurance-based products, creating superior guaranteed returns and results for his clients, resulting in greater retirement income and real wealth.

Although he has been retained in the past to work with advisors from insurance distribution firms with annual sales volumes of $1 to $5 billion, today Matt focuses on a very small and specialized group of asset-management-focused advisors and multidisciplinary law firms. This narrow focus assures the public that any advisor or law firm that has completed the SMART training is properly trained and equipped to help their client Strategically Move Around Retirement Taxation®.

OTHER BOOKS AND
TRAINING BY MATT ZAGULA

Spend It Twice, A Retirees Guide to Free Money: This book is about getting money to the people in our lives that matter. Could be our spouse, our kids, or even a charity—whichever matters most to you. What it is not is a recycled financial book saying the same old stuff. This is straightforward no-nonsense advice that will work in any financial climate. In *Spend It Twice, A Retiree's Guide to Free Money*, Matt Zagula will show you how to create wealth for your family, create income for your surviving spouse, and protect yourself from the financial devastation long-term care can unleash upon you without touching any of your retirement income or retirement savings.

Invasion of the Money Snatchers: Knowledge is power, so arm yourself and prepare for battle! Here is what you must know now! How to avoid paying nasty hidden medical taxes that you didn't have to pay. How gifts to your children can be hazardous to your health and your wealth. Stress-test your money so you can enjoy a stress-free retirement. How to protect your home from future government liens.

Get Smart: The world is full of bold claims. It's also filled with an abundance of disappointment and empty promises. The very idea that you can double your dollars is both attractive and seemingly too good to be true. Think about it, wouldn't it be great to have twice the income and double the value of your life savings for your family? If you dare to dive in to get the "more" that you truly deserve you'll learn exactly how to reclaim profits currently taken by Wall Street banks, their brokerage firms, and large insurance companies and put those dollars where they belong, back in your pocket.

DISCLAIMER

All of the ideas and opinions expressed are the author's. The content within does not constitute and is not meant to serve as individual financial advice. Nor should any of the content presented be considered tax, legal, planning, investment, or accounting advice. This type of service or advice should only be given by a professional advisor obtained by the reader who can review the reader's current and past financial situation as well as assess future goals.

While all facts and numbers have been backed up with sources, the author and publisher make no warranty with respect to accuracy. Author and publisher assume no responsibility for errors and omissions or for any liability, loss, or damages that occur as a result of reading or using the strategies discussed within this book. No guarantees are made to the reader regarding the performance of various investment and insurance products, and all illustrations are hypothetical—provided for educational purposes only, not to solicit sales or make any guarantees.

While the concepts discussed may be appropriate for some individuals, the laws of various states and the rules of various insurers and tax authorities should be considered by the reader and their advisor. While every attempt has been made to provide accurate content, changes in tax rulings, legislation, and regulations may impact the accuracy of the information and numbers presented.

While the illustrations used in this book represent a real, underlying policy, they are still hypothetical and not a guarantee of performance of any individual insurance product. While the company discussed has a strong history of making dividend payments, readers should understand that dividends are not guaranteed. Likewise, the amount of a dividend payment is not guaranteed. Readers must work with their own qualified insurance professional and review individual policy documents to fully understand what they may, and may not, receive should they choose to take out a policy.

As discussed, in order for policy loans to be tax-free, policies must not become modified endowment contracts (MECs). Should a policy become a MEC, as described by federal tax law, any withdrawals or policy loans may be taxable.

Life insurance policies, including those mentioned in this book, require underwriting to ensure overall insurability of the applicant. The author and publishers make no guarantee that the reader will or can qualify for life insurance. They also make no representation that policy terms, benefits, cash values, and premiums will be the same or similar to those presented in the book.